THE COMPLETE BOOK OF CLASSIC

CHEVROLET®

MUSCLE CARS

1955-1974

MIKE MUELLER

motorbooks

Quarto is the authority on a wide range of topics.

Quarto educates, entertains and enriches the lives of our readers—enthusiasts and lovers of hands-on living.

www.quartoknows.com

© 2017 Quarto Publishing Group USA Inc.
Text © 2017 Mike Mueller
Photography © Mike Mueller except where noted otherwise.
First published in 2017 by Motorbooks, an imprint of Quarto Publishing Group USA Inc., 400 First Avenue North, Suite 400, Minneapolis, MN 55401 USA. Telephone: (612) 344-8100 Fax: (612) 344-8692

quartoknows.com
Visit our blogs at quartoknows.com

Motorbooks titles are also available at discounts in bulk quantity for industrial or sales-promotional use. For details contact the Special Sales Manager at Quarto Publishing Group USA Inc., 400 First Avenue North, Suite 400, Minneapolis, MN 55401 USA.

10 9 8 7 6 5 4 3 2 1

ISBN: 978-0-7603-5233-5

Library of Congress Cataloging-in-Publication Data

Names: Mueller, Mike, 1959- author.
Title: The complete book of classic Chevrolet muscle cars : 1955-1974 / Mike Mueller.
Description: Minneapolis, Minnesota : Motorbooks, 2017. | Series: Complete book series
Identifiers: LCCN 2016041172 | ISBN 9780760352335 (hardback)
Subjects: LCSH: Chevrolet automobile--History. | Muscle cars--United States--History. | BISAC: TRANSPORTATION / Automotive / Antique & Classic. | TRANSPORTATION / Automotive / History. | TRANSPORTATION / Automotive / Pictorial.
Classification: LCC TL215.C5 M875 2017 | DDC 629.222--dc23-
LC record available at https://lccn.loc.gov/2016041172

Acquiring Editor: Darwin Holmstrom
Project Manager: Jordan Wiklund
Art Director: James Kegley
Layout: Danielle Smith-Boldt

Printed in China

MIX
Paper from responsible sources
FSC® C016973

General Motors Trademarks used under license to Quarto Publishing Group USA Inc.

Contents

Acknowledgments

I've been writing about cars and photographing them for nearly thirty-five years now because, as one might guess, I'm a car guy. Can't help it. I come from car guys, many of my friends are car guys, and even a couple of my ex-wives were car guys. Any chance I had at growing up to be president surely was dashed when I got that Craftsman toolbox for Christmas about a half-century ago, but no need for condolences. If not for cars, I'd probably be working a real job. Or, more likely, looking for one—as far away from Washington as possible.

Doling out thanks for this carefree career begins with my pa, Jim Mueller Sr., back in Champaign, Illinois, who taught me basic auto mechanics the hard way: "Git 'er done or you don't git anywhere." My brother, Dave, also of Champaign, deserves mucho credit as well for all the inspiration and able-bodied photographic assistance he's supplied over the years, and the same goes for my brother-in-law, Frank Young, of nearby Mahomet. Together, they make up the best free labor pool money can't buy. As for my youngest sibling, Kenny, also based in the Land of Lincoln . . . well, he's one heckuva little brother. And I simply refuse to forget another bro, Jim Mueller Jr., who we lost to cancer in 2014. The game's just not the same without Jimbo playing along.

Meanwhile, here in Arlington, Texas, I would've had a far tougher time missing deadlines if not for the aid of Erin Welker, the greatest car girl in the history of car girls. Erin not only handles a wrench better than most men, but she also reads reasonably well, a talent that often comes in handy considering I can't spell for spit. And I furthermore can't help but wonder if any copy editors out there can do a better Swiss steak . . .

Two other car-Texans, Tom and Michelle Grothouse, from across the cul-de-sac, also deserve kudos for keeping me in the loop concerning the automotive scene here at the northern reaches of the Lone Star State. Now if they'd only buy five copies of this completed epic for Tom's mother, being he's now famous and stuff—at least as far as you're concerned.

Like said career, this book has been many years in the making, both literally and figuratively. Much of the material was first pulled together in 2008 for MBI Publishing's *Complete Book of Classic GM Muscle*, a hefty read that, as its name implied, featured the hottest products offered by Chevrolet, Pontiac, Buick, and Oldsmobile during the 1960s and 1970s. Former MBI editors Lindsay Hitch and Chris Endres were responsible for shepherding those original pages into print, under the direction of longtime friend Zack Miller. Zack then re-tasked me eight years later with repackaging the Chevrolet chapters within the covers you now hold, edited this time by Jordan Wiklund and MBI vet Darwin Holmstrom. Mucho appreciation goes to all three for once more putting up with me. Don't know how y'all do it.

I might also say the following pages began forming about the time Donald Farr gave me my first magazine job with Dobbs Publishing Group in Florida in 1987. There, I was fortunate enough to cross paths with the late Paul Zazarine, who helped make *Muscle Car Review* magazine a force on the automotive newsstand. Paul was always there on the other end of the phone whenever I called for technical support, or just to chat. He's still missed too.

In his stead, I luckily have two other former DPG comrades to fall back on: Steve Statham and Tom Shaw, former editors of *Musclecar Enthusiast* and *Muscle Car Review*, respectively. Don't know what I'd do without these super-duper car dudes, who never fail to respond, with great vigor, to my pleas regarding research help or photographic contributions. Stock photos also came from Hawaiian Bob McClurg and Wisconsin's Mecum Auctions (www.mecum.com), courtesy of John Kraman and Sam Murtaugh. Additional endless appreciation goes to west Texan David Kimball for his incredible cutaway artwork depicting Chevrolet engines from the inside out.

Peggy Kelly and Larry Kinsel up at GM Media Archives in Detroit graciously supplied archival pics (with much haste and little fanfare). Another ol' friend at GM, Global Propulsions Systems Communications man Tom Read, also lent yet another helping hand, as did Christo Datini, archivist extraordinaire at the GM Heritage Center. Former "COPO man" Jim Mattison, now running Pontiac Historic Services (www.phs-online. com), even made the mistake of telling me to call him at home with questions concerning 1969's 427-powered Camaros and Chevelles. Talk about a true car guy.

Various clubs were of priceless help too, as were all the vehicle owners who allowed me to capture their pride and joys (on both film and digital card) over the years while working my way toward this end. This list is too cumbersome for these pages, but I definitely know who all you great car guys (and gals) are. Many thanks to each and every one.

Mike Mueller

Introduction

She's Real Fine

They all reside in museums today: Super Sport Chevelles and Stage 1 Buicks; Z28 Camaros and Boss Mustangs; 409 Chevys and Hemi Mopars; et cetera, et cetera. Long known as muscle cars, high-performance transports like these initially were called supercars a half century ago, and for good reason. No, they couldn't leap tall buildings, in one bound or otherwise. Nor could they outrun a revolver, nor overpower a train. What they could do was send mild-mannered drivers flying, sans nerdy glasses, with but a punch of their right foot. Sure, hot cars were nothing new when Detroit's pioneering muscle-bound models took off. But this new breed maxed out thermometers like never before.

By most accounts, the modern muscle car was born in 1964, the fruit of the Pontiac division's labors. John DeLorean's baby, GTO, instantly inspired various midsized copycats; Oldsmobile's 4-4-2, followed by 1965's Gran Sport from Buick. Next came Chevrolet's original SS 396 Malibu, a limited-edition midyear 1965 offering that started gaining ground on the segment's progenitor in 1966 and eventually replaced it as Detroit's top-selling high-performance vehicle.

Only two mean machines topped the sales charts during America's original muscle car era: the GTO from 1964 to 1968, and Chevelle SS from 1969 to 1973. And while the popularity contest, generally speaking, went to the Pontiac during its 1964 to 1974 run, remember that Chevy didn't even get in the game seriously until 1966, then retired from the race a year later. From 1966 to 1972, midsized SS production was 390,981, compared to 395,127 for the "Goat." But the roles reverse themselves if you concentrate on this epoch's big years, 1969 to 1971, when Super Sports outsold GTOs by 37 percent, 167,972 to 122,986. Talk about your beatdown.

Suffice it to say, numbers alone helped Chevy fans argue that nobody built four-wheeled muscle better during the 1960s and 1970s. Never-ending arguments involving head-to-head runoffs

Super Sport Family Tree	
1961–1968	Impala SS (6-cyl. & V-8)
1963–1976	Nova SS (6-cyl., small- & big-block V-8)
1964–1965	Malibu SS (6-cyl. & small-block V-8)
1965	Z16 Malibu (Chevrolet's first SS 396)
1966–1970	Chevelle SS 396
1967–1972	Camaro SS (small- & big-block V-8)
1967–1969	Impala SS 427
1968–1970	El Camino SS 396
1970–1972	Chevelle SS 454
1970–1972	El Camino SS 454
1970–1971	Monte Carlo SS454
1971–1973	Chevelle SS (small- & big-block V-8)
1971–1988	El Camino SS (small- & big-block V-8)
1983–1988	Monte Carlo SS
1990–1993	454SS pickup
1994–1998	S10 SS compact pickup
1994–1996	Impala SS (Caprice-based)
1996–2002	Camaro SS
2000–2007	Monte Carlo SS
2003–2006	SSR pickup
2003–2006	Silverado SS
2006	Silverado Intimidator SS
2004–2009	Impala SS
2005–2010	Cobalt SS
2006–2007	Malibu & Malibu Maxx SS
2006–2009	Trailblazer SS
2008–2010	HHR SS
2010–	Camaro SS
2014–	Chevrolet SS

Opposite: The muscle car market was home to only two sales leaders during the sixties and early seventies: Pontiac's GTO from 1964 to '68 and Chevrolet's Chevelle SS beginning in 1969. FYI, the '69 SS 396 in the foreground also bested its '69 GTO rival in this vintage drag competition. *Tom Shaw*

aside, no other brand offered as many blood-pumping choices as Chevy. Sexy Super Sport treatments appeared in Impala, Camaro, Nova, El Camino, and Monte Carlo ranks. Non-SS buyers also felt the love, as many of Chevrolet's strongest V-8s appeared optionally for all models, compact Chevy II to full-sizers. Hell, they even turbocharged Corvairs.

Opposite: Chevrolet offered five performance models in 1967, with Corvette joined by four Super Sports: Nova, Chevelle, Impala, and Camaro. *GM*

Below: The original GTO not only established a first-year Pontiac sales record, but it also helped mark a new annual production standard for the entire division in June 1964. At left is general manager Elliot "Pete" Estes, the man who made sure this supposedly taboo machine made it into production. *GM*

RPO Codes

In 1963, Chevrolet revised its regular production option (RPO) language, dropping the three-digit nomenclature used previously in favor of an alpha-numeric list that cleanly broke down the seemingly countless codes into related groups. For example, all Chevy engines were tagged with an "L" prefix, all transmissions with an "M." The really good stuff was found in the "Z" category, labeled "Chevrolet Special Items." Z11, Z16, Z28—you get the picture. Changed and rearranged a few times over the years (among other things, various group counts expanded, and lengthened codes such as"LS6" and "ZR1" appeared), the original RPO structure looked like this a half century back:

Code	Option Group
A01 through D99	Body
F01 to F39	Frame
F40 through F99	Front & rear suspension
G50 through H99	Rear axle
J50 to J99	Brakes
K01 through L99	Engine
M01 to M99	Transmission
N01 to N29	Fuel & exhaust
N30 to N49	Steering
P01 through S99	Wheels & tires
T50 to T59	Sheet metal
T60 through U99	Electrical & instruments
V01 to V29	Radiator and grille
V30 to V99	Bumpers & miscellaneous
Z01 to Z49	Chevrolet Special

590,072

David Kimble

Perusing the company's powertrain menu was no short order either. Still taking down names after kicking tails in its fifth generation, Chevy's so-called small-block V-8 hit its first-gen performance zenith as the seventies opened for business, with 1970's 350-cubic-inch LT-1 making 370 horsepower in Corvette applications, 360 when dropped into that year's remade Z28 Camaro. Another Corvette option, the 350-horsepower L79 327, previously

had put the "shazam" in Chevelle in 1965, and the "too much" in Chevy II in 1966. Apparently size really didn't matter.

Putting the "small" in small-block was its overall dimensions, which were far more compact compared to most other V-8s seen prior to this milestone mill's 1955 introduction. It also was predictably lighter than rivals, and even weighed 42 pounds less than the old, reliable "Stovebolt"

six that had powered all Chevrolets since 1929. Nestled way down there between '55 Bel Air fenders was Chevy's modern overhead-valve (OHV) V-8.

"Small-block" didn't actually enter the automotive lexicon until well after Chevrolet began fostering a big-block counterpart, born in 1958 at 348 cubes. The famed 409's forefather, this W-series engine was followed seven years later

Gen-I Small-Block Family Ties

Five generations have made the scene since Chevrolet's seemingly immortal small-block V-8 debuted for 1955, with the latest, greatest group debuting each time within fiberglass bodywork. The markedly upgraded 5.7-liter Gen-II followed for Corvette only in 1992, then was superseded by the radically redesigned Gen-III five years later, again as the exclusive heart of Chevy's equally eternal two-seater. Horsepower hounds knew the Gen-II and Gen-III V-8s best by their top-shelf RPO tags: LT1 and LS1, respectively. New for 2005, along with the sixth-generation (C6) Corvette, was the LS2 Gen-IV, a 6.0-liter aluminum marvel that put out 400 horsepower. And when the C7 Stingray debuted for 2014, it featured the Gen-V, a 455-horse mill that revived that revered LT1 tag. Now six decades young and counting, the small-block family has experienced various displacement boosts over the years, with 1955's 265-cubic-inch original upstaged by the 283 in 1957, the 327 in 1962, and the 350 in 1967. Three years later came the biggest small-block yet, the 400, which simply wasn't suited for performance applications. Nor was the yeoman 307, offered from 1968 to '73. The Gen-I progression follows here:

Year	RPO	CID	CR	Bore & Stroke	Horsepower	Torque	Valve Sizes
1955	n/a[1]	265	8:1	3.75 × 3.00	162 at 4,400	257 at 2,200	1.72 × 1.30
1957	n/a[1]	283	8.5:1	3.87 × 3.00	185 at 4,600	275 at 2,400	1.72 × 1.30
1962	300	327	10.5:1	4.00 × 3.25	250 at 4,400	350 at 2,800	1.94 × 1.50
1967	L48[2]	350	10.25:1	4.00 × 3.48	295 at 4,800	380 at 3,200	1.94 × 1.50
1967	Z28[3]	302	11:1	4.00 × 3.00	290 at 5,800	290 at 4,200	2.02 × 1.60
1968	n/a[4]	307	9:1	3.87 × 3.25	200 at 4,600	300 at 2,400	1.72 × 1.50
1970	LF6	400	9:1	4.125 × 3.75	265 at 4,400	400 at 2,400	1.94 × 1.60

NOTE: CID is cubic inch displacement; CR is compression ratio; bore & stroke in inches
[1] Base V-8
[2] Camaro SS only
[3] Camaro Z28 only
[4] Base V-8 for full-size Chevys, Chevelle & Nova

Left: Chevy's W-engine legacy began in 1958. Notice the cylinder block deck is inclined, creating combustion chambers within each bore. Displacing 348 cubic inches, this Turbo Thrust V-8 was reserved for high-performance applications only. All versions featured high compression (9.5:1 or better) and dual exhausts, and a four-barrel carburetor was standard. The ultimate rendition was the Super Turbo Thrust, fed by three Rochester two-barrels. *GM*

Opposite: In base form, fed by a two-barrel carburetor, Chevrolet's original small-block V-8 produced 162 horsepower in 1955. Adding a four-barrel carb and dual exhausts boosted output to 180 horses. *David Kimble cutaway, courtesy GM*

Style Matters

When Chevrolet unveiled its reborn LT1 V-8 for 1992's Corvette, eagle-eyed enthusiasts were quick to point out the missing hyphen—the decal last seen on fiberglass hoods twenty years before clearly read "LT-1." But both usages, with hyphen and without, appeared in print back in the seventies, thanks in part to Chevy's own mixed messages. Official RPO listings used LT1 for the engine, while the cars themselves were promoted as LT-1 Corvettes. Before that, RPO Z28 also morphed into Z-28 when the 302-powered Camaro was introduced in 1967, then was recast yet again as Z/28 after badges went onto this hot pony the following year. Later, the advertised name went full circle, back simply to Z28, the reference used throughout this book in the best interests of continuity. Similar varying usages commonly appear whenever historians write about Chevys, hence the prevailing style seen here: no hyphens, just as official options paperwork always spelled it out. The same applies to engine/transmission nomenclature. You'll see both Turbo-Jet (on air cleaner decals, most prominently) and Turbo Jet mentioned in official paperwork, and big-block Turbo Hydra-Matic citations over the years have included Turbo-400 and Turbo 400. Or TH-400, TH 400, and TH400. Again, titles sans hyphens will be the style seen within these covers, if only for simplicity's sake. Historical consistency also comes into play concerning Chevrolet's long-running "mouse motor," now touted formally from corporate sources as the honored "Small Block." But, while it does deserve such capital treatment, you'll see small-block on these pages, per long-standing tradition. Funny thing, though: when the company's world-famous logo is mentioned in GM press releases, a lower-case "b" is almost always present. Capitalization, however, is the order of the day here. After all, it isn't just anyone's neckwear—it's Chevy's Bowtie.

by the even more impressive Mk IV V-8, a large powerplant that took the name game to another level. In slang terms, small-blocks became known on the street as "mouse motors," Mk IVs "rats." Like its W-family predecessors, Mk IV big-blocks existed primarily to fill performance orders. Expansion followed suit as 1965's original

396-cubic-inch Turbo Jet was joined in 1966 by a 427-cubic-inch running mate, then a hefty 454 inches in 1970. King of the 454s was 1970's LS6, the 450-horsepower beast that transformed the new SS 454 Chevelle into what many still believe was the leader of Detroit's original muscle car pack.

Opposite: No engine produced more horses, 450 real ones, during Detroit's original muscle car era than Chevrolet's LS6 454 Turbo Jet, offered only for midsized Super Sports (Chevelle and El Camino) in 1970. A 425-horsepower LS6 was a Corvette-only option in 1971. *David Kimble cutaway, courtesy GM*

Below: The exotic ZL1, an all-aluminum 427-cubic-inch Mk IV big-block, appeared in limited numbers in 1969. Advertised output was a token 430 horsepower. *David Kimble cutaway, courtesy GM*

David Kimble

				Mk IV Big-Block Family Ties				
Year	**RPO**	**CID**	**Bore & Stroke**	**CR**	**Horsepower**	**Torque**	**Carburetor**	**Valve Sizes**
1965	L35	396	4.094 × 3.76	10.25:1	325 at 4,800	410 at 3,200	Quadara-jet 4-barrel	2.06 × 1.72
1966	L72	427	4.250 × 3.76	11:1	425 at 5,600	460 at 4,000	Holley 4-barrel	2.19 × 1.72
1967	L88	427	4.250 × 3.76	12.5:1	430 at 5,200	450 at 4,400	Holley 4-barrel	2.19 × 1.88
1969	ZL1	427	4.250 × 3.76	12:1	430 at 5,200	450 at 4,400	Holley 4-barrel	2.19 × 1.88
1970	L34	402	4.1260 × 3.76	10.25:1	350 at 4,200	415 at 3,400	Quadra-jet 4-barrel	2.06 × 1.72
1970	LS5[1]	454	4.250 × 4.00	10.25:1	360 at 5,400	500 at 3,200	Quadra-jet 4-barrel	2.06 × 1.72
1971	LS6[2]	454	4.250 × 4.00	9:1	425 at 5,600	475 at 4,000	Holley 4-barrel	2.19 × 1.88

NOTE: CID is cubic-inch displacement; RPO is regular production option; CR is compression ratio; bore/stroke & valve sizes (intake × exhaust) in inches
[1]Chevelle version; 1970's Corvette LS5 was advertised at 390 horsepower
[2]LS6 V-8 was only available for Corvette in 1971; it was a 450-horsepower Chevelle-only option in 1970

Above: Corvette has long qualified as a muscle car but is not featured on the following pages because it also always has run in a class all its own. In back is the first of the breed, introduced for 1953 with six cylinders and a Powerglide automatic only. V-8 power saved Corvette from an early death in 1955, and a new body (demonstrated in front here) enhanced the attraction further in 1956.

Opposite: Originally ordered as a Valentine Day's present for his wife, Bob Hamilton's *Red Alert* LS6 SS 454 Chevelle began competing in SS/DA competition in 1970. A year later, the American Model Toy (AMT) company replicated this super stocker in 1/25-scale injection-molded plastic. *Bob McClurg*

"The [LS6] is probably capable of running 13.0s or better [in the quarter-mile] with speeds of 108-110 in pure stock form," claimed a November 1969 *Car Craft* report. "With good tires and some suspension work, the mid-12s should be no sweat." And the same went for upstaging 1970's Hemi 'Cudas, Stage 1 Gran Sports, and Cobra Jet Fords, each a rolling legend in its own right.

The competition was equally historic, if not more so, when Chevrolet's unstoppable small-block was first fired up fifteen years prior. Exciting, new cars were everywhere you looked in 1955, with Chrysler Corporation officials spending a small fortune on sensational restyles for their entire lineup. Low-priced Plymouth especially benefitted from a dose of award-winning good looks, not to mention the installation of its first V-8, also fitted with trendy overhead valves. OHV V-8s debuted for Packard and Pontiac as well in 1955, and Chevy's archrival, Ford, wowed industry watchers with its two-seat Thunderbird, a Corvette knock-off powered by yet another thoroughly modern OHV engine, Dearborn's Y-block V-8, introduced in 1954.

Limited to six cylinders during its first two years on the road, Corvette was surely saved from an early grave by Chevrolet's original small-block, which displaced 265 cubic inches in 1955. Output, in base passenger-car applications, was 162 horsepower, 180 for the optional Super Turbo Fire V-8 with its dual exhausts and Carter four-barrel carburetor. When installed between fiberglass fenders, a more aggressive mechanical can was stuffed in, pumping power production up to 195 horses. Keys behind the release of these ponies included an oh-so-short stroke (3.00 inches) and lightweight ball-stud rocker arms, which worked in concert to help small-blocks wind up like no other engines then running. Commonly credited to Chevrolet today, the ball-stud rocker idea actually came from Pontiac.

When wrapped up in critically acclaimed Bel Air coupe sheet metal, Chevy's headline-making small-block cost about $2,300 in 1955, and that too represented really big news. A triple-digit top-end had never before come this cheap, nor had such a bodacious body. "New" wasn't a big enough word for the totally redesigned automobile that became known simply as "The Hot One."

On the street, this fire-breather was virtually unbeatable. As *Road & Track* explained, "It certainly appears that a Chevrolet V-8 with [the] optional 180 bhp engine and 4.11 axle will out-accelerate any American car on the market today!" Test results were 9.7 seconds for the 0 to 60 run, 17.2 for the quarter mile. Any American car launching from rest to 60 miles per hour in less than 10 seconds in those days represented reason enough to halt the presses.

Right: Corvette V-8s in 1955 received chrome dress-up and a lumpier cam, with the latter addition helping boost output from 180 horsepower to 195. *David Kimble cutaway, courtesy GM*

Opposite: It wasn't broke, but Chevrolet fixed it. A mild restyle and even more small-block power made 1956's Chevy an even hotter proposition. Meanwhile, 1955's model line nomenclature rolled over, with the bare-bones 150 series serving as the base, 210 models representing the next step up, and Bel Airs leading the way.

Below: Chevrolet's totally new 1955 models represented a full-court press of sorts; potential buyers simply had no defense up against this intimidating new player in the low-priced field. While Ed Cole's engineers addressed the nuts and bolts, Clare MacKichan's creative staff handled styling, and their "Futuramic" makeover was every bit as historic as Cole's small-block V-8.

1955 V-8 Bel Air hardtop/convertible

Wheelbase	115 inches
Length	195.6 inches
Width	74 inches
Height	62.1 inches (hardtop)
Weight	3,165 pounds (hardtop), 3,285 pounds (convertible)
Price	$2,166 (hardtop), $2,305 (convertible)
Track	58/58.8 (front/rear, in inches)
Wheels	15-inch
Tires	6.70 × 15
Suspension	independent A-arms, coils springs, stabilizer bar in front; solid axle w/multi-leaf springs in back
Steering	25.7:1 recirculating ball
Brakes	11-inch drums, front/rear
Engine[1]	162-horsepower 265-cubic-inch Turbo Fire V-8 w/2-barrel carb & single exhaust 180-horsepower 265-cubic-inch Turbo Fire V-8 w/4-barrel carb & dual exhausts [1]solid lifters used in manual-trans applications; hydraulic lifters used when optional Powerglide automatic installed
V-8 cam specs	solid: 0.336-inch lift intake, 0.334 exhaust; 246-degrees duration (intake/exhaust) hydraulic: 0.334-inch lift (intake/exhaust) & 302-degrees duration (intake/exhaust)
Transmission	3-speed, standard; overdrive & Powerglide automatic, optional

"Loaded for bear" was *Road & Track*'s description for 1955's 195-horsepower Corvette, which did 0 to 60 in 8.7 ticks, the quarter mile in 16.5. "The V-8 engine makes this a far more interesting automobile and has upped performance to a point at least as good as anything in its price class," added Ken Fermoyle in *Motor Life*. And this was only the beginning.

Super Turbo Fire output increased to 205 horsepower in 1956, inspiring *Mechanix Illustrated* scribe Tom McCahill to label this year's strongest mainstream Chevy the "best performance buy in the world." But he spoke too soon. Nineteen-fifty-six's restyled Corvette was treated to two even warmer small-blocks, one fed by a single four-barrel and rated at 210 horsepower, the other featuring dual fours and advertised at 225 horses. According to *Sports Car Illustrated*'s Roger Huntington, the 225-horsepower 265 represented "one of the hottest production engines in the world—regardless of piston displacement." McCahill then raised the bar even higher, proclaiming that it "might very well be rated the greatest competition engine ever built."

Right: The Corvette's solid-lifter, dual-carb V-8, rated at 225 horsepower, became a passenger-car option midyear in 1956.

Below: Ramjet fuel injection, supplied by Rochester, became an option for all Chevrolet cars in 1957, including the last of the two-door Nomad wagons.

Opposite: Originally known simply as "Black & Whites," for obvious reasons, Chevrolet's race-ready 1957 models were later nicknamed "Black Widows." They were prepped at Chevrolet's SEDCO (short for Southern Engineering Development Company) race shop, officially listed as a division of Nalley Chevrolet, Inc., of Atlanta, Georgia. Both sedan and convertible Black Widows (with fuel-injected or dual-carb V-8s) were built.

Chevrolet officials fanned the flames further in January 1956, announcing they also would offer the Corvette's twin-carb small-block as a passenger-car option, resulting in what McCahill called "a poor man's answer to a hot Ferrari." "Zero to 30 averages 2.3 seconds, 0–60 8.9 seconds, and in 12 seconds, you're doing 70," he continued after pouring the coals to a 225-horsepower Bel Air. "This is about May, June, and July faster than the Chevrolets of just two or three years ago."

A third Corvette V-8, fitted with a high-lift camshaft developed by chief engineer Zora Arkus-Duntov (and hence tabbed the "Duntov cam"), also appeared in

1956 but was specified for "racing purposes only." Unofficial output was 240 horsepower.

Proving there's never a substitute for cubic inches, Chevrolet dealt its first-generation small-block a displacement boost in 1957, increasing bore from 3.75 inches to 3.875, resulting in 283 cubes. Along with a stroke stretch (to 3.25 inches), a second bore job five years later produced the 327 small-block, which required a recast block to allow for 4.00-inch cylinder diameters. And another enlarged stroke (3.48 inches) followed in 1967 to create the 350 Turbo Fire V-8, offered exclusively along with that year's new Camaro SS, detailed in Chapter 4.

Back in 1957, Chevy's 283 V-8 produced 270 horses when fed by dual carbs. But, once again, there was more. Available for all models that year was the hottest small-block yet, a 283 crowned by Ramjet fuel injection. Supplied by Rochester, this equipment did existing carburetors one better by, among other things, delivering said fuel in a heartbeat. Throttle response was superb. In *Road & Track*'s words, "the fuel injection engine is an absolute jewel, quiet and remarkably docile when driven gently around town, yet instantly transformable into a roaring brute when pushed hard."

Chevrolet's Hottest Small-Block V-8s, 1955–1969

Year	RPO	CID	CR	Horsepower	Torque	Induction	Valve Sizes
1955	410	265	8:1	195 at 5,000	260 at 3,000	Carter 4-bl	1.72 × 1.50
1956	411[1]	265	9.25:1	225 at 5,200	270 at 3,600	2 Carter 4-bls	1.72 × 1.50
1957	578[2]	283	10.5:1	283 at 6,200	290 at 4,400	fuel injection	1.72 × 1.50
1961	354	283[3]	11:1	315 at 6,200	295 at 5,000	fuel injection	1.72 × 1.50
1962	582	327[3]	11.25:1	360 at 6,000	352 at 4,000	fuel injection	2.02 × 1.60
1964	L76	327[3]	11:1	365 at 6,200	350 at 4,000	Holley 4-bl	2.02 × 1.60
1965	L84	327[3]	11:1	375 at 6,200	352 at 4,600	fuel injection	2.02 × 1.60
1966	L79	327	11:1	350 at 5,800	360 at 3,600	Holley 4-bl	2.02 × 1.60
1967	L48	350	10.25:1	295 at 4,800	380 at 3,200	Quadra-jet 4-bl	1.94 × 1.50
1967	Z28	302	11:1	290 at 5.800	290 at 4,200	Holley 4-bl	2.02 × 1.60
1969	L46	350[3]	11:1	350 at 5,600	380 at 3,600	Quadra-jet 4-bl	1.94 × 1.50
1970	LT-1	350[3]	11:1	370 at 5,800	380 at 4,000	Holley 4-bl	2.02 × 1.60
1970	Z28	350	11:1	360 at 6,000	380 at 4,000	Holley 4-bl	2.02 × 1.60

NOTE: RPO is regular production option; CID is cubic inch displacement; CR is compression ratio; valve sizes in inches (intake × exhaust)
[1]Passenger-car option; RPO 469 in Corvette
[2]Passenger-car option; RPO 579D in Corvette
[3]Corvette only (briefly offered as Chevelle option in 1964 then cancelled)

Opposite: Prior to the 350-cubic-inch LT-1, introduced for 1970 at 370 horsepower, Chevrolet's hottest carbureted small-block was the L76 327, first offered as a 365-horsepower Corvette option in 1964. *GM*

Left: Along with Chevy's 283 Ramjet V-8, Black Widows also featured various chassis modifications, including heavy-duty six-lug truck hubs and wheels. Notice the header-type split exhaust manifolds and special induction ductwork.

Below: Nineteen-fifty-eight's bigger, heavier Chevys required bigger, stronger engines to stay in the race, hence the need for the 348-cubic-inch W V-8. New badges debuted this year too, with the pecking order now consisting of Del Ray, Biscayne, and Bel Air. A fourth model, Impala, also was introduced as a subset of the Bel Air line. Powering this topless Impala is a triple-carb Super Turbo Thrust 348.

Two injected 283s (rated at 250 and 283 horsepower, respectively) debuted in 1957. The 250-horsepower relied on a hydraulic cam and 9.5:1 compression, while the fiercer "fuelie" featured the mechanical Duntov bumpstick and 10.5:1 compression. Fuel injection remained available in passenger-car ranks up through 1959, and Corvettes continued the legacy into 1965. Explaining why the fuelie 'Vette retired was simple: cost.

Chevrolet's big-block legacy dated back to 1958, the year a new lineup (Biscayne, Bel Air, Impala) debuted consisting of models that were notably larger and heavier than 1957's 150/210/Bel Air trio. Physical laws being the same in most states, these heftier Chevys needed a bit more engine to keep up the pace, hence the logic behind the 348-cubic-inch Turbo Thrust's introduction.

Originally conceived with both auto and truck duty in mind, the 348 represented Chevrolet's strongest passenger-car option each year from 1958 into early 1961. All varieties featured high compression (9.5:1 or better), all relied on at least a four-barrel carb, and all had dual exhausts. Ultimate Super Turbo Thrust renditions relied on solid lifters and three Rochester two-barrel carburetors. Maximum advertised output during the four-year 348 run was 350 horsepower.

Innovative staggered valves were what helped the 348 make so much hay, and this was made possible by the use of the same ball-stud rocker

1958 Impala	
Model availability	2-door sport coupe & convertible
Wheelbase	117.5 inches
Length	209 inches
Width	77.7 inches
Height	55.8 inches (sport coupe)
Weight	3,684 pounds (hardtop w/348 V-8)
Price	$2,693 (V-8 sport coupe), $2,841 (V-8 convertible)
Track	58.8 (front/rear, in inches)
Wheels	14-inch
Tires	8.00 × 14
Suspension	independent A-arms, coils springs & stabilizer bar in front; upper/lower control arms & coil springs in back
Steering	recirculating ball
Brakes	4-wheel drums
Available V-8s	185-horsepower 283-cubic-inch Turbo Fire V-8 w/2-barrel carburator & single exhaust 230-horsepower 283-cubic-inch Super Turbo Fire V-8[1] w/4-barrel carburetor 250-horsepower 348-cubic-inch Turbo Thrust V-8[1] w/4-barrel carburetor 280-horsepower 348-cubic-inch Super Turbo Thrust V-8[1] w/triple carburetors 315-horsepower 348-cubic-inch Super Turbo Thrust V-8[1] w/triple carburetors 250-horsepower 283-cubic-inch Ramjet V-8[1] w/Rochester fuel-injection 290-horsepower 283-cubic-inch Ramjet V-8[1] w/Rochester fuel-injection [1]w/dual exhausts NOTE: 185-horsepower/230-horsepower/250-horsepower F.I. 283s & 250-horsepower 348 had hydraulic cam; 280-horsepower/315-horsepower 348s & 290-horsepower 283 F.I. had solid-lifter high-lift cam.
Transmission	Standard 3-speed manual, w/all V-8s
Optional	Overdrive (w/Super Turbo Fire V-8); Powerglide automatic (w/Super Turbo Fire V-8); Corvette-type Powerglide automatic (w/283 F.I. & 250-horsepower 348); Turboglide automatic (w/250- & 280-horsepower 348); close-ratio 3-speed manual (all V-8s)

Right: Four 348 V-8s were offered in 1958, beginning with a 250-horsepower Turbo Thrust topped by a Carter four-barrel carburetor. Next up was the 280-horsepower Super Turbo Thrust with triple carbs and hydraulic lifters. At the top was the 315-horsepower Super Turbo Thrust featuring solid lifters and 11:1 compression. A Police Special version of the latter 348 also appeared with a four-barrel in place of those three Rochester two-barrels.

Opposite top: Superseding Bel Air as Chevrolet's flagship in 1958, the chrome-encrusted Impala was only offered in two sexy fashions: sport coupe and convertible. An exclusive roofline set the Impala hardtop apart from its Bel Air counterpart, and a flashy tri-tone interior was standard inside. Impalas also received six taillights in back, compared to four for other 1958 models.

Opposite bottom: The 348 V-8 also served well as a truck power source, as this 1960 Spartan Model 80 attests. *GM*

1958–1961 348-cubic-inch W-engines

Year	RPO	Cam	CR	Horsepower	Torque	Induction	Valve Sizes
1958	576A	hydraulic	9.5:1	250 at 4,400	355 at 2,800	Carter 4-barrel	1.94 × 1.66
	573A	hydraulic	9.5:1	280 at 4,800	355 at 3,200	3 Rochester 2-barrels	1.94 × 1.66
	573B[1]	solid	11:1	315 at 5,600	356 at 3,600	3 Rochester 2-barrels	1.94 × 1.66

[1]A "Police Special" version of this V-8, fitted with a 4-barrel carb, also was released in 1958

Year	RPO	Cam	CR	Horsepower	Torque	Induction	Valve Sizes
1959	576A	hydraulic	9.5:1	250 at 4,400	355 at 2,800	Carter 4-barrel	1.94 × 1.66
	573A	hydraulic	9.5:1	280 at 4,800	355 at 3,200	3 Rochester 2-barrels	1.94 × 1.66
	576B	solid	11:1	305 at 5,600	350 at 3,600	Carter 4-barrel	1.94 × 1.66
	573B	solid	11:1	315 at 5,600	356 at 3,600	3 Rochester 2-barrels	1.94 × 1.66
	577	solid	11.25:1	320 at 5,600	358 at 3,600	Carter 4-barrel	1.94 × 1.66
	574	solid	11.25:1	335 at 5,800	358 at 3,600	3 Rochester 2-barrels	1.94 × 1.66

Year	RPO	Cam	CR	Horsepower	Torque	Induction	Valve Sizes
1960	576A	hydraulic	9.5:1	250 at 4,400	355 at 2,800	Carter 4-barrel	1.94 × 1.66
	573A	hydraulic	9.5:1	280 at 4,800	355 at 3,200	3 Rochester 2-barrels	1.94 × 1.66
	576B	solid	11:1	305 at 5,600	350 at 3,600	Carter 4-barrel	1.94 × 1.66
	577[2]	solid	11.25:1	320 at 5,600	358 at 3,600	Carter 4-barrel	1.94 × 1.66
	574[2]	solid	11.25:1	335 at 5,800	358 at 3,600	3 Rochester 2-barrels	1.94 × 1.66

[2]RPOs 577 & 574 superseded by RPOs 590 & 571, respectively, on April 1, 1960

Year	RPO	Cam	CR	Horsepower	Torque	Induction	Valve Sizes
1961	576A[3]	hydraulic	9.5:1	250 at 4,400	355 at 2,800	Carter 4-barrel	1.94 × 1.66
	573A[3]	hydraulic	9.5:1	280 at 4,800	355 at 3,200	3 Rochester 2-barrels	1.94 × 1.66
	572[4]	solid	11:1	305 at 5,600	350 at 3,600	Carter 4-barrel	1.94 × 1.66
	590[4]	solid	11.25:1	340 at 5,800	362 at 3,600	Carter 4-barrel	2.07 × 1.72
	573B[4]	solid	11.25:1	350 at 6,00	364 at 3,600	3 Rochester 2-barrels	2.07 × 1.72

[3]Not available w/1961 Impala SS
[4]Available w/1961 Impala SS

NOTE: RPO is regular production option; CR is compression ratio; valve sizes in inches (intake × exhaust); bore & stroke was 4.125 × 3.25 inches
All 348 V-8s featured dual exhausts.

Right: Chevrolet began installing Borg Warner four-speeds sticks in Corvettes in 1957, and some dealers apparently also started swapping floor-shifted four-gears into passenger cars then too. Shown here is Chevy's first factory direct mainstream four-on-the-floor, which appeared in small numbers in 1959. Reportedly, these installations were performed quite crudely, with the opening in the transmission tunnel burned through like it was performed seconds before quitting time.

Opposite: Notice the fender badges (behind the headlights) on this Impala convertible. Reportedly, only about twenty-five Chevy passenger cars were built with optional fuel injection in 1959.

arm design pioneered by Chevrolet and Pontiac three years before. These individually mounted rockers allowed engineers to position valves where they would work best: intakes were located up high near the intake manifold runners, exhausts were found down low, close to the exhaust manifolds. This distinctive zigzag layout in turn improved overall flow by lessening passage wall area inside the ports.

Equally distinctive were the W-engine's combustion chambers, which resided inside the cylinder bores, not in the heads. The working face of the 348 head was basically flat (valves opened and closed in slight pockets), while combustion chambers were created in the bores by sloping each cylinder bank's deck down at a 16-degree angle off perpendicular. This left a wedge-shaped "squish area" between piston and head at top dead center.

An idea basically borrowed from Mercedes, this design reportedly simplified production and allowed the use of larger valves due to revised geometry. The angled deck surfaces transformed the upper bore openings from circles into ellipses, which translated into increased cross-sectional bore area. More bore cross-section meant more room for larger-diameter valves.

Rated at 250 horsepower in base form featuring a single Carter four-barrel, the 348 powered Chevrolet's flagships into 1961 before reaching early retirement. After revisiting their drawing boards late in 1960, W-series engineers then came back with the 409, the drag strip sensation popularized in song by The Beach Boys in 1962.

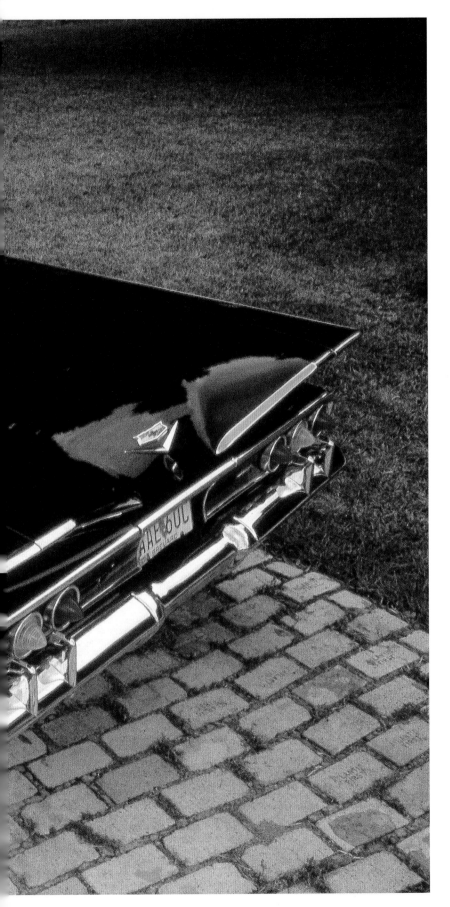

Above: Fuel injection remained available in passenger-car ranks up through 1959, and Corvettes continued the legacy on into 1965. Maximum FI output was 283 horsepower in 1957, 290 in 1958, 315 in 1961, and 360 in 1962, the first year for the 327-cubic-inch small-block. The Ramjet V-8's zenith, 375 horses, arrived in 1964.

Left: Those love-'em-or-hate-'em bat wings, introduced out back for 1959, reappeared the following year for yet another notably restyled Chevrolet. The top power option for 1960's Impala was a 335-horsepower 348 Super Turbo Thrust.

WHEN BIG WAS BEST

Full Size Muscle: 1961–1969

► Only Chevrolet's two W-series V-8s, 348- and 409-cubic-inch, were available for the first Impala SS in 1961.

► Both six-cylinders and small-block V-8s became available for Chevy's second-edition Super Sport in 1962.

► The Impala SS graduated up into full model-line status in 1964.

► Chevrolet's 409 V-8 retired in 1965, the same year the new Mk IV big-block debuted.

► The SS 427 joined the base Impala Super Sport in 1967.

► Chevrolet offered the SS 427 only for 1969, the full-sized Super Sport's final year.

► Now based on the four-door Caprice, a reborn Impala SS was offered from 1994 to 1996, with power coming from the Corvette's 5.7-liter LT-1 V-8.

Chevrolet's decision to revive its revered Impala SS nameplate in 1994 after a quarter-century in the archives instantly reminded many among the Chevy faithful of better days, a time before federal mandates governed what we could drive, and a period predating the magical moment when gasoline morphed into gold. These were the free-to-be-me sixties, a decade that began in a rush as Detroit's horsepower race took a new turn only to run afoul of Washington's ever-tightening safety standards and emissions restrictions. Signs pointing to the end of the road for America's original muscle car—be it compact, intermediate, or full-sized—were already apparent by 1969, and it was all over but the shouting within a couple years. While the seventies started out high-powered, they quickly fizzled, then went completely cold as far as four-wheeled fun was concerned.

Above: Chevrolet's famed 409 V-8 was already making big noise on America's drag strips when The Beach Boys popularized it lyrically in 1962. Optional dual carburetors were first offered atop the 409 late in 1961 and then became a full-fledged RPO the following year.

Previous pages: Left: Full-sized performance was on the way out when Chevrolet introduced its SS 427 Impala in 1967. As the name implied, this big bully came only with the most cubic inches Chevy offered at the time. *Tom Shaw Right:* Chevrolet's Super Sport legacy runs back to 1957, when Zora Arkus-Duntov (at the wheel here) attempted to take the international racing world by storm with his magnesium-bodied XP-64 racer, identified on paper as a Corvette SS. Reportedly, Duntov was asked if this exotic machine was a sports car. "No, it's a *Super Sports* car." *GM*

Opposite: Chevrolet's Impala SS debuted early in 1961 along with the 409. Most Super Sports built that first year featured 348 V-8s, as demonstrated here. Notice the absence of an engine badge on the front fender.

Not only did 1969 signal the end of the hottest decade then on record in automotive annals, it also represented the final fling for Chevrolet's first-gen Impala Super Sport, one of the sixties' sweetest rides. Born midyear in 1961, when big cubes in a big car stood as a leadfoot's sole choice, the Impala SS debuted primarily as a real fine showcase for the equally new 409 V-8. But eight years later, this sexy legacy was discontinued. The market for full-sized performance cars had been sinking steadily following Pontiac's introduction of midsized muscle in 1964. With the groundbreaking GTO on the scene, joined immediately by various carbon copies, the new logic was painfully plain: why board a big-ticket luxury liner when you could spend far less for a cozier cabin cruiser and usually make more waves in the process? At least it was fun while it lasted, especially for Chevy bean

counters, who gleefully watched some 920,000 Impala SS coupes and convertibles sail during that celebrated 1961–1969 run.

Of course, not every full-sized SS was truly a performance car. In 1962, Chevrolet began allowing six-cylinders and 283 small-blocks into the mix in order to widen the car's appeal. Limited production in 1961 was a mere 456. The count then soared to more than 99,000 in 1962, then peaked at 243,000 for 1965, the same year the 409 was replaced by Chevy's new Mk IV big-block.

Every first-year Super Sport built, on the other hand, was able to back up its pizzazz with a real punch. Only Chevrolet's two biggest, baddest V-8s were available in 1961: the aforementioned 409, rated at 360 horsepower, and its 348-cubic-inch W-series brethren, then playing its swan song. While many witnesses considered the former to

1961-1965 409 V-8s

Year	Production	RPO	Horsepower	Torque	CR	Carburetor	Valve Sizes
1961	142	580	360 at 5,800	409 at 3,600	11.25:1	Carter 4-barrel	2.07 × 1.72
1962	15,019	580	380 at 5,800	420 at 3,200	11:1	Carter 4-barrel	2.19 × 1.72
		587	409 at 6,000	420 at 4,000	11:1	2 Carter 4-barrels	2.19 × 1.72
1963	16,902	L33	340 at 5000	420 at 3,200	10:1	Rochester 4-barrel	2.07 × 1.72
		L31	400 at 5,800	425 at 3,600	11:1	Carter 4-barrel	2.19 × 1.72
		L80	425 at 6,000	425 at 4,200	11:1	2 Carter 4-barrels	2.19 × 1.72
		Z11*	430 at 6,000	n/a	13:1	2 Carter 4-barrels	2.19 × 1.72
		*Race-only V-8 that displaced 427 cubic inches due to lengthened (3.65 inches) stroke					
1964	8,864	L33	340 at 5,000	420 at 3,200	10:1	Rochester 4-barrel	2.07 × 1.72
		L31	400 at 5,800	425 at 3,600	11:1	Carter 4-barrel	2.19 × 1.72
		L80	425 at 6,000	425 at 4,200	11:1	2 Carter 4-barrels	2.19 × 1.72
1965	2,828	L33	340 at 5,000	420 at 3,200	10:1	Rochester 4-barrel	2.07 × 1.72
		L31	400 at 5,800	425 at 3,600	11:1	Carter 4-barrel	2.19 × 1.72

NOTE: RPO is regular production option code; CR is compression ratio; valve sizes in inches (intake × exhaust)
Bore & stroke was 4.3125 × 3.50 inches; all 409s used solid-lifter cams except for the L33

be little more than a bored/stroked update of the latter, the transformation was nowhere near that simple.

For starters, punching out the 348 represented a risky proposition—not enough iron existed between the water jacket and cylinder bore. Accordingly, the block was recast, allowing bore diameter to increase from 4.125 to 4.3125 inches without fear of compromising cylinder walls. At the same time, stroke was stretched a quarter inch to 3.50, resulting in the displacement figure that fit so well into The Beach Boys' hit lyrics.

Plenty of modifications were made from there, so much so that swapping parts between 348 and 409 basically was out of the question. New forged-aluminum pistons featured centered wrist pins and symmetrical valve reliefs milled straight across the piston top in pairs. Their 348 counterparts had offset wrist pins with one large intake relief and one smaller relief. This meant a 348 required two opposite sets of four pistons, each set with its own part number. All 409 pistons interchanged regardless of which cylinder bank they went into. Cylinder heads closely resembled the 348 design

but were specially cast to accept larger-diameter pushrods and machined on top for heavier valve springs. Valve sizes stayed the same, but the cam was a far more aggressive solid-lifter unit.

Supplying air/fuel was a large Carter AFB four-barrel on an aluminum intake. Foregoing the 348's triple-carburetor setup, engineers turned to a single unit that basically matched the 348's trio in flow while meeting NASCAR's mandate labeling multiple-carb arrangements illegal for stock car racing. From there, a Delco-Remy dual-breaker distributor sparked the mixture, and low-restriction header-style exhaust manifolds hauled away by-products.

Although Chevy's latest, greatest W engine was available in any 1961 model, wrapping one up in SS garb was a no-brainer. "Put the big 409 into the new Super Sport and you have one of the hottest test cars of the season," claimed a *Motor Trend* report. "When I floored it in second, I got the impression that Chevrolet had made a mistake in labeling this car a Super anything," added *Motor Trend*'s Bob Ames. "They should have called it the Incredible Impala!"

Above: **Super Sport Impalas fitted with 409s in 1961 were adorned with appropriate fender badges.**

Opposite: **Three 348 V-8s were available beneath SS Impala hoods in 1961—two with single four-barrel carburetors, one with three two-barrels. Advertised output for the triple-carb version was 350 horsepower.**

1961

Chevrolet's Super Sport kit was first announced to dealers late in January 1961. A fact-filled amendment to that year's *Passenger Car Specifications* book followed in February, and color brochures officially introduced the deal to the public, though not without some confusion. This option was reportedly available for all Impala models except the Nomad station wagon. Two-door or four, sedan, coupe, or convertible, each variety supposedly could've been tricked out in SS trim. But no 1961 Super Sport sedans or four-doors were built.

The SS kit alone cost a mere $53.80, and for that tidy sum a 1961 Impala was adorned with exclusive spinner wheel covers and appropriate badges. Added inside were a Corvette-style grab bar on the dashboard's far right and a bright floor plate for the shifter in four-speed models.

Various other regular production options were mandatory. A customer also had to shell out for RPO 200 (heavy-duty shock absorbers), RPOs 253 and 593 (heavy-duty springs front and rear, respectively), RPO 324 (power steering), RPO 412 (power brakes), RPO 331 (7,000-rpm tachometer, mounted on the steering column), RPO 427 (padded instrument panel), RPO 686 (police car metallic brake linings), and RPO 691 (8.00 × 14

1961 IMPALA SS

Model availability	2-door sport coupe & convertible
Wheelbase	119 inches
Length	209.3 inches
Width	78.4 inches
Height	55.5 inches
Curb weight	3,480 pounds
Price	SS "kit" cost $53.80; various mandatory options pushed total price to about $3,700
Track	60.3/59.3 (front/rear, in inches)
Wheels	14 × 6 stamped-steel
Tires	8.00 × 14 4-ply w/narrow whitewalls
Suspension	independent upper/lower A-arms, heavy-duty coils springs, stabilizer bar in front; 4-link control arms & heavy-duty coil springs in back; heavy-duty shock absorbers
Steering	power-assisted recirculating ball
Brakes	power-assisted drums w/sintered metallic linings, front/rear
Engines	305-horsepower 348-cubic-inch Turbo Thrust V-8 (RPO 572)
	340-horsepower 348-cubic-inch Turbo Thrust V-8 (RPO 590)
	350-horsepower 348-cubic-inch Turbo Thrust V-8 (RPO 573B)
	360-horsepower 409-cubic-inch Turbo Fire V-8 (RPO 580)
Compression	9.5:1, 305-horsepower 348; 11.25:1, 340/350-horsepower 348s & 360-horsepower 409
Transmissions	4-speed manual, standard; Powerglide automatic optional only w/305-horsepower 348 V-8

four-ply tires with narrow whitewalls). Available only for the Impala SS in 1961, those tires were mounted on station-wagon rims that measured 1 inch wider than the 14 × 5 wheels found on other Chevy passenger cars that year.

Along with the 360-horsepower 409 (RPO 580), three 348s were available beneath the 1961 Super Sport's hood. Two (RPOs 572 and 590) were topped by single Carter four-barrels, while the third (RPO 573B) was crowned with three Rochester two-barrels. Outputs were 305 (RPO 572), 340 (RPO 590), and 350 (RPO 573B) horsepower. Transmission choices numbered two: a heavy-duty Corvette-type Powerglide automatic (RPO 313) or a four-speed manual (RPO 685). The 'Glide was only available behind the 305/348, while the 340- and 350-horsepower versions were limited to the four-speed, which in this case relied on a 2.54:1 first gear. The 409's close-ratio four-speed featured a 2.20:1 low.

Opposite: A tachometer and a passenger-side grab bar were standard inside 1961's Impala SS, as was a bright floor plate for manual transmission models.

Below top: All full-sized Chevrolets—Impala, Bel Air, Biscayne—could be equipped with the 409 during its 1961 to 1965 run. This 1962 Bel Air is powered by the 409-horsepower dual-carb version.

Below bottom: Originally a high-profile, high-performance machine, the Impala SS became available with all engines, including mundane six-cylinders, in 1962. Both convertibles and hardtops again were offered. *GM*

1962 IMPALA SS

Model availability . . . . 2-door sport coupe & convertible
Wheelbase . . . . 119 inches
Length . . . . 209.6 inches
Width . . . . 79 inches
Height . . . . 55.5 inches (coupe)
Curb weight . . . . 3,750 pounds (coupe w/409 V-8)
Price . . . . RPO 240 SS trim package cost $53.80 (plus $102.25 for bucket seats)
Track . . . . 60.3/59.3 (front/rear, in inches)
Wheels . . . . 14 × 6
Tires . . . . 7.00 × 14 (coupe); 7.50 × 14 (convertible)
Suspension . . . . independent A-arms, coils springs & stabilizer bar in front; 4-link control arms
& coil springs in back
Steering . . . . recirculating ball; power-assist, optional
Brakes . . . . 11-inch drums, front/rear; power-assist, optional
Engines . . . . 135-horsepower 235-cubic-inch 6-cylinder w/1-barrel carburetor, standard
170-horsepower 283-cubic-inch Turbo Fire V-8 w/2-barrel carburetor, standard
250-horsepower 327-cubic-inch Turbo Fire V-8 w/4-barrel carburetor, optional
300-horsepower 327-cubic-inch Turbo Fire V-8 w/4-barrel carburetor, optional
380-horsepower 409-cubic-inch Turbo Fire V-8 w/4-barrel carburetor, optional
409-horsepower 409-cubic-inch Turbo Fire V-8 w/2 4-barrel carburetors, optional
Compression 8.25:1, 6-cyl.; 8.5:1, 283 V-8; 10.5:1, 327 V-8s; 11:1, 409 V-8s
Transmissions . . . . 3-speed manual, standard; 4-speed (n/a behind 6-cyl.) & Powerglide automatic,
optional (4-speed only w/409 V-8s)

1962

The RPO 580 V-8 returned for 1962, bringing 380 horses along with it this time. A second W-motor (RPO 587) also appeared, fitted with dual Carter carburetors, which apparently found their way atop a few 409s late in the 1961 run via an over-the-counter Service Package dealer option. RPO 587 output was 409 horsepower. Again, 409s were available for all full-size Chevys in 1962, SS or not.

Yet another little-known Service Package was released on August 1, 1962, consisting of weight-saving body parts (hood and inner/outer fenders stamped in aluminum), just the things to help a Biscayne, Bel Air, or Impala reach the far end of a quarter mile a little quicker. A second race-only package followed two weeks later for the 409 V-8, this one featuring a hotter cam, radical raised-port cylinder heads, and a revised two-piece dual-carb intake needed to mate up with those taller heads. The manifold's lower section served as a valley cover, while the high-rise upper half handled fuel delivery. No one knows exactly how many of these tall-port 409s were installed late in 1962; common estimates claim no more than twenty.

Back on the street, 1962's SS package, now labeled RPO 240, was attractively enhanced with anodized body-side spears and a swirl-pattern insert for the rear cove panel. Bucket seats were

now included inside, but the big news came under the hood. Two base engines were offered this time: a 135-horsepower 235-cubic-inch six-cylinder and a 170-horsepower 283-cubic-inch V-8, the former fed by a one-barrel carb, the latter a two-barrel. Along with the two 409s, options included a pair of new-for-1962 327-cubic-inch small-blocks, one

(RPO 300) rated at 250 horsepower, the other (RPO 397) at 300.

A mundane column-shifted three-speed manual was standard behind the base six and three small-blocks, while it was once more four gears only for the W big-block. The Powerglide automatic again was optional, for all but the two 409s.

Above: The supreme 409 was the Z11 rendition, built for racing only. Displacing 427 cubic inches, thanks to a stroker crank, the Z11 featured special raised-port heads that mandated the installation of a two-piece intake manifold.

Opposite: Chevrolet released various race-ready goodies for its full-sized flyers during the summer of 1962. Among these were aluminum body parts, created to save weight on the strip. This veteran quarter-miler has those rare aluminum components.

1963 IMPALA SS

Model availability . . . . 2-door sport coupe & convertible
Wheelbase . . . . 119 inches
Length . . . . 210.4 inches
Width . . . . 79 inches
Height . . . . 55.5 inches (coupe)
Curb weight . . . . 3,877 pounds (coupe w/409 V-8)
Price . . . . RPO Z03 SS package cost $161.40
Track . . . . 60.3/59.3 (front/rear, in inches)
Wheels . . . . 14 × 6
Tires . . . . 7.00 × 14 (coupe); 7.50 × 14 (convertible); 8.00 × 14 (w/409 V-8)
Suspension . . . . independent A-arms, coils springs & stabilizer bar in front; 4-link control arms
& coil springs in back
Steering . . . . recirculating ball; power-assist, optional
Brakes . . . . 11-inch drums, front/rear; power-assist, optional
Engines . . . . 140-horsepower 230-cubic-inch 6-cylinder w/1-barrel carburetor, standard
195-horsepower 283-cubic-inch Turbo Fire V-8 w/2-barrel carburetor, standard
250-horsepower 327-cubic-inch L30 Turbo Fire V-8 w/4-barrel carburetor, optional
300-horsepower 327-cubic-inch L74 Turbo Fire V-8 w/4-barrel carburetor, optional
340-horsepower 409-cubic-inch L33 Turbo Fire V-8 w/4-barrel carburetor, optional
400-horsepower 409-cubic-inch L31 Turbo Fire V-8 w/4-barrel carburetor, optional
425-horsepower 409-cubich-inch L80 Turbo Fire V-8 w/2 4-barrel carburetors, optional
Compression . . . . 8.5:1, 6-cyl.; 9.5:1 283 V-8; 10.5:1, 327 V-8s; 10:1, L33 409; 11:1, L31 & L80 409s
Transmissions . . . . 3-speed manual, standard; 4-speed (n/a behind 6-cyl.) & Powerglide, optional
(4-speed only w/L31 & L80 409s; 4-speed & Powerglide available behind L33 409)

1963

Revised RPO codes debuted this year, with the base 409, now rated at 400 horsepower, listed as the L31 V-8. Boosted up to 425 horses, the dual-carb 409 took on the L80 tag, and a third variant, the L33, also appeared. This police option V-8, advertised at 340 horsepower, featured a single Rochester four-barrel, a relatively mild hydraulic cam, a softened 10:1 squeeze, and a 409 first: an optional Powerglide automatic. All other 409s were delivered with sticks only.

Another new RPO, Z11, picked up where 1962's two Service Packages left off. Priced at a formidable $1,237, the Z11 deal (formally known as the Special Performance Equipment Package) added another aluminum nose (plus aluminum bumpers), a close-ratio Borg-Warner T-10 four-speed, sintered metallic brakes with special cooling gear for the rear drums, a heavy-duty Positraction axle with 4.11:1 gears, and the raised-port 409, which didn't actually displace 409 cubic inches. A stroke increase to 3.65 inches translated into 427 cubes for 1963's Z11 V-8, which also featured 13.5:1 compression and a special cowl-induction air cleaner that helped suck in cooler, denser outside atmosphere from the high-pressure area at the base of the windshield. Chevrolet paperwork claimed the Z11 409 made 430 horsepower, but those in the know knew better—more than 500 ponies surely were present.

1963 Z11

Body modifications	hood, hood catch, grille filler panel, fenders, bumpers & bumper brackets all made of weight-saving aluminum; some cars featured deleted sound deadener, insulation, and heater
Wheelbase	119 inches
Length	210.4 inches
Width	79 inches
Height	55.5 inches
Curb weight	3,405 pounds
Price	RPO Z11 cost $1,237
Track	60.3/59.3 (front/rear, in inches)
Wheels	15 × 5.5 stamped-steel
Tires	6.70 × 15 bias ply
Suspension	independent upper/lower A-arms, heavy-duty coil springs in front; 4-link control arms & heavy-duty coil springs in back; heavy-duty shock absorbers (front stabilizer bar deleted)
Steering	recirculating ball
Brakes	11-inch drums w/sintered metallic linings, front/rear (special cooling equipment for rear drums)
Engine	430-horsepower 427-cubic-inch "W" V-8 w/raised-port heads & 2-part intake manifold
Bore & stroke	4.3125 × 3.65 inches
Compression	13.5:1
Fuel delivery	2 Carter 4-barrel carburetors w/ cowl-induction air cleaner
Transmission	Borg-Warner T-10 4-speed manual
Rear axle	4.11:1 Positraction

Opposite: The label on this rare factory drag car's fender reads "Aluminum—Do Not Touch." Weight-saving body parts were included along with the Z11 409 V-8 in 1963. *Bob McClurg*

Below: Widening the full-sized Super Sports scope in 1962 sent sales soaring—to 99,311 that year, 153,271 in 1963. This 1963 SS sport coupe is powered by a 283 small-block V-8.

Type	CID	Mark Motors Description	Notes
Mk I	427 409-based "W" V-8	Made hay In super-stock & F/X drag racing	
Mk II	409	"Porcupine-head" V-8	Precursor to "Mystery Motor"
Mk IIS	427	Stroked "Mystery Motor"	Turned heads at Daytona in February 1963
Mk III	500	Design study that investigated feasibility of expanding displacement up to 500 cubes	Never made it off drawing board
Mk IV	396	Available for Corvette (425 horsepower), Z16 Malibu (375 horsepower), and full-sized Chevys (325/425 horsepower) in 1965	Displacement increased to 427 in 1966 and 454 in 1970

Fifty-seven Z11 Chevys were reportedly released in 1963, and more might have made it into drag racers' hands had GM not issued its anti-racing decree in January. Down the tubes, almost overnight, went Zora Duntov's Grand Sport Corvettes, Pontiac's Super Duty Catalinas, and Chevrolet's Z11. Killed off at the same time was another 427-cubic-inch big-block that surely would have rewritten NASCAR record books had it had the chance.

Primarily the work of Dick Keinath, this mean mill began taking shape in July 1962 and was originally called the Mk II V-8 after the 409 breed was tabbed Mk I. Although the two distant relatives did share displacement levels early on, the Mk II represented a notable departure, resembling the W engine only slightly on the bottom end. Keinath then developed a stroker crank that maximized cubes to take full advantage of NASCAR's 427-cubic-inch limit,

inspiring a new name in the process: Mark IIS, "S" for stroked.

Heads for the Mk II/Mk IIS also featured staggered valves on individual ball-stud rockers, but they were canted at odd angles toward their ports, resulting in arguably the best breathing characteristics achieved to that point from a Detroit V-8. The varying angles at which the valve stems protruded upward in turn resulted in an apt nickname: "porcupine" heads.

Above: Chevrolet engineers showed up at Daytona in February 1963 with a big-block V-8 soon known as the "Mystery Motor." This 427-cubic-inch engine produced upwards of 520 horsepower and posted speeds of 165 miles per hour on Daytona's high banks. *GM*

Left: Chevrolet's Mk IIS V-8 earned its "Mystery Motor" nickname because NASCAR rivals at Daytona in February 1963 didn't know what had hit them. According to legendary race car builder Smokey Yunick, it was "probably the best engine I ever saw come out of Detroit." *David Kimble cutaway, courtesy GM*

Opposite: Anyone could have walked into any Chevy dealership during the early sixties and ordered a 409 V-8 in the model or body of his or her choice—hence this four-door Impala, which features a 425-horsepower 409.

According to racing legend Smokey Yunick, only forty-two 427-cubic-inch MK IIS V-8s were manufactured, just enough to allow Chevrolet to go stock car racing in 1963. Dyno tests reportedly claimed 520 horsepower for the engine dubbed the "Mystery Motor" after it showed up that year at Daytona and wowed witnesses with unheard-of speeds in excess of 165 miles per hour. A Mystery Motor Chevy won both 100-mile Daytona 500 qualifiers that year, but mechanical failures allowed Fords to dominate the big show.

Making far less noise this year were the 5 extra horses supplied by the latest Super Sport's new 230-cubic-inch six-cylinder, a major improvement over the aging 235-cubic-inch Stovebolt it replaced. Upgraded too was 1963's standard SS small-block, which featured a compression boost from 8.5:1 to 9.5:1. Still a two-barrel 283, it now produced 195 horsepower. Relabeled L30 and L74, 1962's two optional 327s rolled over unchanged at 250 and 300 horsepower, respectively. The SS package itself, now listed under RPO Z03, also repeated in nearly identical fashion. Swirl-pattern instrument panel inserts flanking the steering column were new inside, as was a full-length console for automatic and four-speed models.

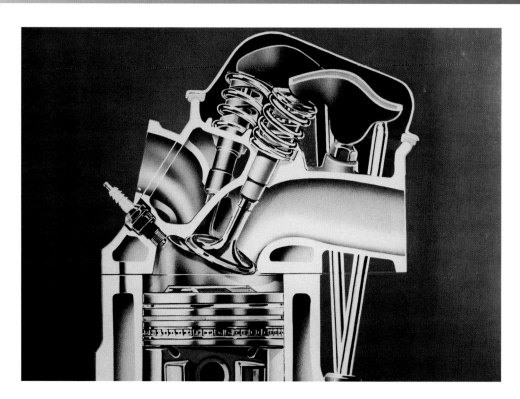

1964 IMPALA SS

Model availability	2-door sport coupe & convertible
Wheelbase	119 inches
Length	209.8 inches
Width	77 inches
Height	55.1 inches (coupe)
Curb weight	3,325 pounds (6-cyl. coupe); 3,450 pounds (V-8 coupe); 3,435 (6-cyl. convertible); 3,555 pounds (V-8 convertible)
Price	$2,839 (6-cyl. coupe); $2,947 (V-8 coupe); $3,068 (6-cyl. convertible); $3,196 (V-8 convertible)
Track	60.3/59.3 (front/rear, in inches)
Wheels	14 × 6
Tires	7.00 × 14 (coupe); 7.50 × 14 (convertible); 8.00 × 14 (w/409 V-8)
Suspensions	independent A-arms, coils springs & stabilizer bar in front; 4-link control arms & coil springs in back
Steering	recirculating ball; power-assist, optional
Brakes	11-inch drums, front/rear; power-assist, optional
Engines	140-horsepower 230-cubic-inch 6-cylinder w/1-barrel carburetor, standard
	195-horsepower 283-cubic-inch Turbo Fire V-8 w/2-barrel carburetor, standard
	250-horsepower 327-cubic-inch L30 Turbo Fire V-8 w/4-barrel carb, optional
	300-horsepower 327-cubic-inch L74 Turbo Fire V-8 w/4-barrel carb, optional
	340-horsepower 409-cubic-inch L33 Turbo Fire V-8 w/4-barrel carb, optional
	400-horsepower 409-cubic-inch L31 Turbo Fire V-8 w/4-barrel carb, optional
	425-horsepower 409-cubic-inch L80 Turbo Fire V-8 w/2 4-barrel carbs, optional
Compression	8.5:1, 6-cyl.; 9.5:1 283 V-8; 10.5:1, 327 V-8s; 10:1, L33 409; 11:1, L31 & L80 409s
Transmissions	3-speed manual, standard; 4-speed (n/a behind 6-cyl.) & Powerglide automatic, optional (4-speed only w/L31 & L80 409s; 4-speed & Powerglide available behind L33 409)

Above: Many Chevy fans today still feel 1964's Impala SS was the finest of the line, especially so when fitted with a 409, like this convertible.

Opposite top: Key to the Mystery Motor's success (as well as that of the Mk IV big-block to follow) were its free-breathing cylinder heads, nicknamed "porcupines" for the manner in which their valves protruded upward in haphazard fashion.

Opposite bottom: A police option 409 appeared in 1963 and carried on up through 1965. Rated at 340 horsepower, this rather mild rendition was available with an optional Powerglide automatic. All other 409s were limited to four-speed manual installations.

1964

Previously created by checking off an RPO, Chevrolet's full-sized Super Sport officially graduated into a formal model line this year and remained available in hardtop or convertible forms. Trademark swirl patterns continued to appear within the body-side spears, rear cove, and instrument panel, and nearly all other SS features also carried over from 1963. The engine lineup repeated exactly, with those three familiar 409s again leading the way in the power department.

1965 IMPALA SS

Model availability	2-door sport coupe & convertible
Wheelbase	119 inches
Length	213 inches
Width	79.6 inches
Height	54.5 inches (coupe)
Curb weight	3,435 pounds (6-cyl. coupe); 3,570 pounds (V-8 coupe); 3,505 pounds (6-cyl. convertible); 3,645 (V-8 convertible); 3,885 pounds (coupe w/409 V-8)
Price	$2,839 (6-cyl. coupe), $2,947 (V-8 coupe); $3,104 (6-cyl. convertible), $3,212 (V-8 convertible)
Track	62.5/62.4 (front/rear, in inches)
Wheels	14 × 6
Tires	7.35 × 14 (coupes w/base engines); 7.75 × 14 (convertibles & all models w/optional 327 V-8s); 8.25 × 14 (w/optional 409 & 396 V-8s)
Suspension	independent A-arms, coils springs & stabilizer bar in front; 4-link control arms & coil springs in back
Steering	recirculating ball; power-assist, optional
Brakes	11-inch drums, front/rear; power-assist, optional
Engines	140-horsepower 230-cubic-inch 6-cylinder w/1-barrel carburetor, standard
	150-horsepower 250-cubic-inch L22 6-cyl. w/1-barrel carburetor, optional[1]
	195-horsepower 283-cubic-inch Turbo Fire V-8 w/2-barrel carburetor, std.
	220-horsepower 283-cubic-inch L77 Turbo Fire V-8 w/4-barrel carb, optional[1]
	250-horsepower 327-cubic-inch L74 Turbo Fire V-8 w/4-barrel carb, optional
	300-horsepower 327-cubic-inch L74 Turbo Fire V-8 w/4-barrel carb, optional
	325-horsepower 396-cubic-inch L35 Turbo Jet V-8 w/4-barrel carb, optional[1]
	425-horsepower 396-cubic-inch L78 Turbo Jet V-8 w/4-barrel carb, optional[1]
	340-horsepower 409-cubic-inch L33 Turbo Fire V-8 w/4-barrel carb, optional
	400-horsepower 409-cubic-inch L31 Turbo Fire V-8 w/4-barrel carb, optional
	[1]introduced in February 1965
Compression	8.5:1, 230-cubic-inch 6-cyl.; 9.5:1, L22 6-cyl.; 9.25:1, 195-horsepower 283 V-8, L77 283 & L30 327; 10.5:1, L74 327; 10.25:1, L35 396; 11:1, L78 396 & L31 409; 10:1, L33 409
Transmissions	3-speed manual, standard; 4-speed (n/a behind 6-cyl.), optional; Powerglide & Turbo Hydra-Matic (n/a behind 6-cyl. & 283/327 V-8s) automatics, optional (manual trans only behind L78 396 & L31 409; Powerglide available behind L33 409)

1965

A fully freshened, squeaky-clean full-sized Chevy debuted in 1965 to help enhance Super Sport impressions to all-new heights, along with sales. Gone were the swirl-pattern exterior treatments first seen in 1962. Bucket seats carried over inside, but this time the standard console featured a clock, mounted ahead of the shifter in automatic applications, behind when a four-speed was installed. Full instrumentation also replaced idiot lights, with read-outs for oil, amps, and coolant temp appearing in a round pod to the speedometer's left. An identical pod on the right housed a vacuum gauge, which was traded out for a rev counter whenever the U16 tachometer option was specified.

Base engines rolled over into 1965 and were joined by various new options, beginning with a 150-horsepower 250-cubic-inch powerplant. Fed by a four-barrel carb, Chevrolet's L77 283 also joined the L30 and L74 327s on the extra-cost list. But only the two single-carb 409s (L31 and L33) were offered in 1965, the last year for fabled mill that had much of America singing its praises in 1962.

Superseding the 409 midyear was the new Mk IV big-block, a 396-cube Mystery Motor derivative created by cutting the Mk II's bore from 4.25 inches to 4.09. Introduced in February 1965, the 396 Turbo Jet appeared in three forms: the Corvette's 425-horsepower L78, the 375-horsepower L37 for the new SS 396 Malibu, and the 325-horsepower L35 for full-sized models. The brutish L78 also was available for big Chevys.

New, too, for 1965 was Chevrolet's three-speed Turbo Hydra-Matic automatic, offered along with the veteran two-speed Powerglide behind the hydraulic-lifter L35 big-block. The solid-lifter L78, meanwhile, was limited to a stick.

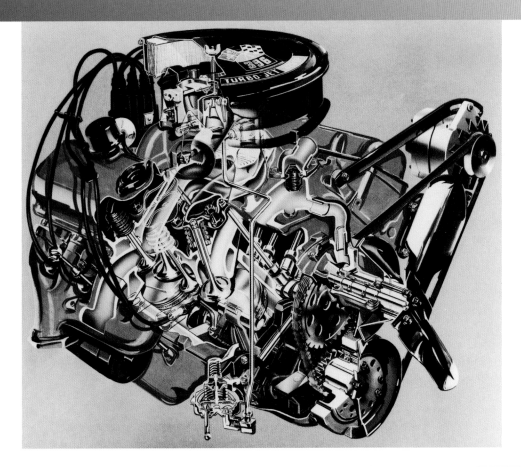

Left: Chevrolet introduced its Mk IV big-block in February 1965. Three 396 Turbo Jets were initially offered; a 425-horsepower version for the Corvette and full-sizers, 375 horses for the new Malibu SS 396, and 325 for big Chevys.

Opposite: Chevrolet discontinued the 409 early in 1965 to make room for its new Mk IV big-block, displacing 396 cubic inches. Super Sport Impalas were fitted with both old and new big-blocks that year; this convertible features the 340-horsepower 409.

Below: Like the 409 before it, Chevrolet's Mk IV big-block was available in all full-sized models, SS or not. The 396 Turbo Jet shown here resides beneath a 1965 Caprice hood. *Tom Shaw*

1966 IMPALA SS

Model availability	2-door sport coupe & convertible
Wheelbase	119 inches
Length	213.1 inches
Width	79.6 inches
Height	54.5 inches (coupe)
Curb weight	3,460 pounds (6-cyl. coupe), 3,485 pounds (V-8 coupe), 3,505 pounds (6-cyl. convertible), 3,630 pounds (V-8 convertible)
Price	$2,842, (6-cyl. coupe), $2,947 (V-8 coupe), $3,093(6-cyl. coupe), $3,199 (V-8 convertible)
Track	62.5/62.4 (front/rear, in inches)
Wheels	14 × 6
Tires	7.35 × 14 (coupes w/base engines); 7.75 × 14 (convertibles); 8.25 × 14 (w/optional 396/427 V-8s)
Suspension	independent A-arms, coils springs & stabilizer bar in front; 4-link control arms & coil springs in back
Steering	recirculating ball; power-assist, optional
Brakes	11-inch drums, front/rear; power-assist, optional
Engines	155-horsepower 250-cubic-inch 6-cyl. w/1-barrel carburetor, standard
	195-horsepower 283-cubic-inch Turbo Fire V-8 w/2-barrel carburetor, standard
	220-horsepower 283-cubic-inch L77 Turbo Fire V-8 w/4-barrel carb, optional
	275-horsepower 327-cubic-inch L30 Turbo Fire V-8 w/4-barrel carb, optional
	325-horsepower 396-cubic-inch L35 Turbo Jet V-8 w/4-barrel carb, optional
	380-horsepower 427-cubic-inch L36 Turbo Jet V-8 w/4-barrel carb, optional
	425-horsepower 427-cubic-inch L72 Turbo Jet V-8 w/4-barrel carb, optional
Compression	8.5:1, 6-cyl.; 9.25:1, 283 V-8s; 10.25:1, 327, L35 396 & L36 427s; 11:1, L72 427
Transmissions	3-speed, standard; 4-speed (n/a behind 6-cyl.) & Powerglide automatic, optional; Turbo Hydra-matic, optional w/396 & L36 427 V-8s (manual trans only behind L72 427)

Above: Two Mk IV V-8s were available in 1966, the carryover 396 Turbo Jet and its 427-cube big brother. Once again, big-block availability extended to all model lines, as well as body styles. This 1966 Impala features the L72 427 Turbo Jet. *Tom Shaw*

Opposite top: Impala SS sales peaked at 243,114 in 1965 and then slowly eased downhill from there. This 327-powered coupe was one of 119,314 Super Sports built for 1966. *GM*

Opposite bottom: An aluminum intake was installed atop 1966's new L72 427, rated at 425 horsepower. *Tom Shaw*

1966

Minor styling updates at the nose and tail and dash/console revisions inside announced the 1966 Super Sport's arrival. Under the hood, 1965's 195-horsepower 283 base V-8 returned, but the 250-cubic-inch inliner, up-rated to 155 horsepower, was the new base six. The L77 283 and L30 327 (now producing 275 horses) remained on the options list, as did the L35 396 Turbo Jet. Gone were the L74 327 and L78 396, although no one missed the latter thanks to the arrival of the 427 Turbo Jet, created by restoring the Mystery Motors' original bore diameter. Two 427s were offered, the 390-horsepower L36 and the intimidating solid-lifter L72, rated the same as 1965's L78: 425 horsepower.

1967

Another new Impala body appeared in 1967, and Super Sports again soldiered on in familiar fashion, though with fewer power choices. Base engines for six and V-8 models rolled over from 1966, as did 1967's three optional eights: the L30 327, L35 396, and L36 427. Now rated at 385 horsepower, the L36 Turbo Jet could be combined with RPO Z24 to create the new SS 427, available in coupe and convertible forms just like their garden-variety SS siblings. The Z24 package included a stiffened suspension, redline tires on 14 × 6 rims, and an exclusive doomed hood adorned with simulated air ducts done in bright aluminum. Also like all 1967 Super Sports, the SS 427 featured blackout treatments for the grille, lower body trim, and rear cove panel.

1967 IMPALA SS 427

Model availability	2-door sport coupe & convertible
Wheelbase	119 inches
Length	213.2 inches
Width	79.9 inches
Height	54.4 inches (coupe)
Curb weight	3,835 pounds (coupe)
Price	RPO Z24 cost $403.30
Track	62.5/62.4 (front/rear, in inches)
Wheels	14 × 6 (15-inch Rally rims included w/optional front disc brakes)
Tires	8.25 × 14
Suspension	independent A-arms, heavy-duty coils springs & stabilizer bar in front; 4-link control arms & heavy-duty coil springs in back; heavy-duty shock absorbers
Steering	recirculating ball; power-assist, optional
Brakes	11-inch drums, front/rear (J52 power front discs, optional)
Engine	385-horsepower 427-cubic-inch L36 Turbo Jet V-8 w/Rochester 4-barrel carb
Transmissions	3-speed manual, standard; 4-speed & Turbo Hydra-Matic automatic, optional

1967 Impala SS Powertrains

Engines	155-horsepower 250-cubic-inch 6-cyl. w/1-barrel carburetor, standard
	195-horsepower 283-cubic-inch Turbo Fire V-8 w/2-barrel carburetor, standard
	275-horsepower 327-cubic-inch L30 Turbo Fire V-8 w/4-barrel carburetor, optional
	325-horsepower 396-cubic-inch L35 Turbo Jet V-8 w/4-barrel carburetor, optional
	385-horsepower 427-cubic-inch L36 Turbo Jet V-8 w/4-barrel carburetor, optional[1]
	[1]included with SS 427 (RPO Z24) package
Compression	8.5:1, 6-cyl.; 9.25:1, 283 V-8; 10:1, L30 327; 10.25:1, L35 & L36 Turbo Jets
Transmissions	3-speed manual, standard; 4-speed (n/a behind 6-cyl.) & Powerglide automatic, optional; Turbo Hydra-Matic automatic, optional behind L35 & L36 Turbo Jets

Right: Standard beneath the SS 427's domed hood in 1967 was Chevrolet's 385-horsepower L36 427 Turbo Jet.

Opposite top: The SS 427 joined the Super Sport Impala lineup in 1967 in both coupe and convertible forms. Along with standard big-block power, the SS 427 also featured a heavy-duty suspension and redline tires on 14 × 6 rims.

Opposite bottom: After selling 2,124 SS 427 coupes and convertibles in 1967, Chevrolet moved another 1,778 out the door the following year. Exclusive exterior identification was again present on all four body sides.

1968

Model line status ended this year as buyers again had to check off RPO Z03 to add Super Sport imagery to their Impala sport coupes and convertibles. According to Chevrolet paperwork, both the Z03 and returning Z24 packages also were available for the new Impala Custom coupe, which featured the luxury-minded Caprice's formal roofline. Some 1968 Impalas also appeared with hideaway headlights, a new option that, according to factory sources, was only available for the top-shelf Caprice. Standard SS 427 stuff this time included a black-accented grille, vertical fender louvers, and 15-inch wheels. Fourteen-inch rims remained the norm for basic Super Sports.

Most of 1967's SS engine lineup carried over, identically spec'ed, save for the base 283 V-8, which was replaced by a 307-cubic-inch small-block, rated at 200 horsepower. Two 327s were optional in 1968, as the L30 was now accompanied by the 250-horsepower L73. The 385-horsepower L36 remained both the heart of the SS 427 and an option for other models, and it was rejoined by RPO L72, the 425-horsepower 427.

1968 IMPALA SS 427

Model availability	2-door coupe & convertible
Wheelbase	119 inches
Length	215 inches
Price	RPO Z24 cost $358.10
Track	62.5/62.4 (front/rear, in inches)
Wheels	15 × 6 (15-inch Rally rims included w/optional front disc brakes)
Tires	G70 × 15 redline
Suspension	independent A-arms, heavy-duty coils springs & stabilizer bar in front; 4-link control arms & heavy-duty coil springs in back; heavy-duty shock absorbers
Steering	recirculating ball; power-assist, optional
Brakes	drums, front/rear (J52 power front discs, optional)
Engines	385-horsepower 427-cubic-inch L 36 Turbo Jet V-8 w/4-barrel carb, standard; 425-horsepower 427-cubic-inch L72 Turbo Jet V-8 w/4-barrel carb, optional
Transmissions	3-speed manual, standard; 4-speed & Turbo Hydra-Matic automatic, optional

1968 Impala SS Powertrains

Engines	155-horsepower 250-cubic-inch 6-cyl. w/1-barrel carburetor, standard
	200-horsepower 307-cubic-inch V-8 w/2-barrel carburetor, standard
	250-horsepower 327-cubic-inch L73 Turbo Fire V-8 w/4-barrel carburetor, optional
	275-horsepower 327-cubic-inch L30 Turbo Fire V-8 w/4-barrel carburetor, optional
	325-horsepower 396-cubic-inch L35 Turbo Jet V-8 w/4-barrel carburetor, optional
	385-horsepower 427-cubic-inch L36 Turbo Jet V-8 w/4-barrel carburetor, optional[1]
	425-horsepower 427-cubic-inch L72 Turbo Jet V-8 w/4-barrel carburetor, optional
	[1]included with SS 427 (RPO Z24) package
Compression	8.5:1, 6-cyl.; 9:1, 307 V-8; 8.75:1, L73 327; 10:1, L30 327; 10.25:1, L35 & L36 Turbo Jets; 11:1, L72 427
Transmissions	3-speed manual, standard; 4-speed (n/a behind 6-cyl.) & Powerglide automatic, optional; Turbo Hydra-Matic 350 automatic, optional behind 283/327 V-8s; Turbo Hydra-Matic 400 automatic, optional behind Turbo Jets

1969

Product planners opted to only offer the SS 427 Impala for 1969, and did so with far less fanfare. A blacked-out grille and familiar SS badges (sans engine identification) represented the only outward clues to the Z24 package's presence—no more domed hood or fender "gills." Interested onlookers even had to squint to make out those small 427 badges hidden, as in 1968, atop the side-marker lights on each front fender.

Beneath that flat hood was again the L36 big-block, now rated at 390 horsepower thanks to mildly modified pistons and heads. Returning as well were heavy-duty underpinnings and Wide Oval redline rubber. Again, the rare L72 427 Turbo Jet also was available at extra cost, this time to help send this boulevard brute off into the history books with a bang.

1969 IMPALA SS 427

Model availability	2-door sport coupe, Custom coupe & convertible
Wheelbase	119 inches
Length	215.9 inches
Price	RPO Z24 cost $422.35
Track	62.5/62.4 (front/rear, in inches)
Wheels	15-inch stamped steel, standard; 15-inch Rally rims, optional
Tires	G70 × 15 redline
Suspension	independent A-arms, heavy-duty coil springs & stabilizer bar in front; 4-link control arms & heavy-duty coil springs in back; heavy-duty shock absorbers
Steering	recirculating ball; power-assist, optional
Brakes	power-assisted front discs; rear drums
Engines	390-horsepower L36 427-cubic-inch Turbo Jet V-8 w/hydraulic lifters
	425-horsepower L72 427-cubic-inch Turbo Jet V-8 w/solid lifters
Compression	10.25:1 (L36); 11:1 (L72)
Fuel delivery	Rochester Quadra-jet 4-barrel carburetor (L36); Holley 4-barrel carburetor (L72)
Transmission	heavy-duty 3-speed, standard; close- & wide-ratio 4-speeds, Turbo Hydra-Matic, optional

1961–1969 Impala SS Production Figures

Year	RPO Breakdowns	Sport Coupe	Convertible	Total
1961	body style breakdown not available			456
1962	RPO 240 (body style breakdown not available)			99,311
1963	RPO Z03 (body style breakdown not available)			153,271
1964	body style breakdown not available			185,325
	L74 300-horsepower 327 Turbo Fire, for all full-sized models			50,150
1965	body style breakdowns not available			243,114
	L74 300-horsepower 327 Turbo Fire, for all full-sized models			56,499
	L35 325-horsepower 396 Turbo Jet, for all full-sized models			55,454
	L78 425-horsepower 396 Turbo Jet, for all full-sized models			1,838
1966		103,442[1]	15,872[2]	119,314
	[1]included 823 6-cylinders, 102,619 V-8s			
	[2]included 89 6-cylinders, 15,783 V-8s			
	L35 325-horsepower 396 Turbo Jet, for all full-sized models			105,844
	L36 390-horsepower 427 Turbo Jet, for all full-sized models			3,287
	L72 425-horsepower 427 Turbo Jet, for all full-sized models			1,856
1967		64,387[3]	9,545[4]	73,932
	SS 427 (RPO Z24, for Impala sport coupe & convertible)			2,124
	[3]included 329 6-cylinders, 64,058 V-8s			
	[4]included 46 6-cylinders, 9,499 V-8s			
	L35 325-horsepower 396 Turbo Jet, for all full-sized models			61,945
	L36 385-horsepower 427 Turbo Jet, for all full-sized models			4,337
1968	RPO Z035			36,432
	SS 427 (RPO Z24)[5]			1,778
	L35 325-horsepower 396 Turbo Jet, for all full-sized models			55,190
	L36 385- horsepower 427 Turbo Jet, for all full-sized models			4,071
	L72 425-horsepower 427 Turbo Jet, for all full-sized models			568
	[5]for Impala sport coupe, Custom coupe & convertible; body style breakdowns not available			
1969	SS 427 (RPO Z24, for Impala sport coupe, Custom coupe & convertible; body style breakdowns not available)			2,455
	L36 390-horsepower 427 Turbo Jet, for all full-sized models			5,582
	L72 425-horsepower 427 Turbo Jet, for all full-sized models			546
	LS1[6] 335-horsepower 427 Turbo Jet, for non-SS models			18,308
	[6]not listed as an SS 427 option, but Z24 installations apparently were possible			

NOTE: See page 32 for 409 V-8 production totals

Left: The standard Mk IV big-block for the last of the big Super Sports was rated at 390 horsepower in 1969.

Opposite: Chevrolet offered its full-sized Super Sport for the last time in 1969. While both the SS 427 and simple Super Sports were seen in 1967 and 1968, only the former was around when the story came to a close.

STAR POWER

Nova SS/COPO: 1963–1971

Americans really didn't know they needed smaller, cheaper automobiles before Chevrolet and Ford rolled out all-new compacts nearly sixty years ago. But boy did we want 'em once Corvair and Falcon appeared—so much so Chevy product planners wasted little time creating a second little car to help meet the growing demand. A decision was made to add a fourth model to the Chevy lineup just two months after the air-cooled Corvair was introduced on October 2, 1959. This new compact then went from drawing board to reality in a scant eighteen months, making this one of the quickest development sagas in GM's storied history. New-for-1962 Chevy II models started rolling off the assembly line in August 1961.

▶ The new-for-1962 Chevy II was Chevrolet's second model to use unitized body/frame construction, following Corvair, introduced two years prior.

▶ Chevrolet began offering an over-the-counter V-8 swap kit for Chevy II early in 1962.

▶ Chevrolet's hottest factory-delivered compact in 1962 was the new Corvair Spyder, powered by a 150-horsepower turbocharged six-cylinder.

▶ In 1963, Nova became the second Chevrolet to join the Super Sport fraternity. The Nova SS legacy ran up through 1976.

▶ A convertible Nova SS was offered for one year only, 1963.

▶ Both the Nova sport coupe and Super Sport models initially failed to return for 1964, but were reinstated midyear by popular demand.

▶ A factory-installed optional V-8 was introduced in 1964.

▶ The Nova SS 396 was built from 1968 to 1970.

▶ The Rally Nova was offered for two years: 1971 and 1972.

▶ Chevrolet's original Nova retired after 1979.

Like the car itself, the name came about in rapid-fire fashion. Most rumors around Detroit in 1961 had the new compact wearing the Nova badge, which had been glowing brightly around the division's experimental studios dating back to 1955. But even most blind men noticed that this noun didn't begin with a C, the prerequisite for Chevrolet monikers during the sixties. With no better candidates in the offing, Chevy II plain and simply emerged at the last minute to handle identification chores. Nova, meanwhile, stuck around to grace the Chevy II's top-shelf sub-series and then became the sole tagline for the entire lineup in 1969.

Debuting on September 29, 1961, Chevy II shared none of its structure with any other GM product. Its conservatively styled, yet crisp three-box unit-body shell featured an isolated subframe up front (bolted to the body in fourteen places) and a rear suspension consisting of a typical live axle held in place by single-leaf springs called mono plates. Measuring 5 feet in length, each mono plate was rolled from high-strength chromium-steel bar stock and used rubber-bushing mounts at both ends to insulate the unitized body from road

shocks. Advantages also included less unsprung weight (one strong leaf weighed less than a typical stack of steel leaf springs), lower manufacturing costs (one single leaf springs was simpler than many clamped together), and improved rust resistance (those stacked leafs always trapped moisture in between them).

Power came from another exclusive, a new inline four-cylinder, Chevrolet's first four-holer since 1928. This frugal mini-motor displaced a meager 153 cubic inches and produced 90 horsepower. An equally new 120-horsepower six-cylinder (that shared various internal components with its smaller running mate) was optional for the Chevy II, standard for the topline Nova.

Setting the 1962 Nova further apart from its plain-Jane brethren were extra trim, upgraded upholstery, and larger tires. Two-door sport coupe and convertible models also were exclusive to the high-grade line. Veteran *Mechanix Illustrated* road-tester Tom McCahill drove the Nova ragtop and came away quite happy: "With a little hopping up, a stick shift and its low price, it should sell like a cold beer on a hot Fourth of July."

Above: Brutish SS 396 Novas were a force to be reckoned with from 1968 to 1970. A 1970 rendition roasts the weenies here. *Bob McClurg*

Previous pages: Left: Chevy II debuted for 1962 as a slight step up from Chevrolet's truly compact Corvair. Top of the Chevy II line was the deluxe Nova rendition, offered only with six-cylinder power. A convertible also was exclusive to the Nova group. *GM*

Right: The hottest compact in General Motors' ranks prior to 1964 was the Corvair Spyder, a turbocharged machine introduced for 1962. The Spyder's force-red pancake six produced 150 horsepower during its short run. A 1964 Spyder appears here.

Opposite: Nova became the second Chevrolet to wear SS badges in 1963. Six-cylinders only were offered beneath the SS Nova's hood that year. *GM*

Chevrolet began handling hop-up chores the following year, when the popular Chevy II returned looking basically the same save for a few trim updates and some interior freshening. A Nova Super Sport debuted in 1963 and was also available as a convertible. Extending the SS touch into compact ranks was a no-brainer, especially after market reactions in 1962 had demonstrated an interesting trend. Of the 326,607 Chevy IIs sold that first year, 59,741 were upscale Nova sport coupes and 23,741 were carefree Nova convertibles. Apparently not all Chevy II buyers minded doling out a few more bucks for a little added flair.

Adding the SS package, RPO Z03, in 1963 required an extra $161. Unlike the first full-sized Super Sport deal two years before, the new Z03 option was an appearance package, beginning with Nova SS emblems on the deck lid and both rear quarters, special bodyside moldings with silver inserts, and a bright insert added to the cove panel in back. Bigger 14-inch wheels (13-inchers were standard for the Chevy II) were a mandatory option for the 1963 Nova SS, and those rims were hidden with the same spinner wheel covers seen on that year's Impala Super Sport.

Interior additions included all-vinyl upholstery, bucket seats, SS identification on the steering wheel, Nova SS on the glove box, an electric clock, and bright instrument panel trim. Real gauges for oil, electrics, and water temperature replaced the Chevy II's idiot lights within that panel. Powerglide-equipped SS Novas were further adorned with a floor shifter surrounded by a bright dress-up plate. Base three-speed examples used a yeoman column shift.

Like all 1963 Novas, the SS was available with only one power source, the purely practical 120-horsepower 194-cubic-inch six. Customers who noticed that the Chevy II engine bay had been designed all along to accept the Bowtie small-block could've swapped in the 283- or 327-cube V-8 with relative ease beneath the nearest shade tree. Or they could have paid big bucks to have their local dealer install Chevrolet's own V-8 conversion kit—the going rate was $1,500 *plus* labor, or more than half of what an entire Chevy II cost. Few opted for this expensive transformation, meaning nearly all early Nova Super Sports struggled to get out of their own way.

No, Chevy's latest SS obviously wasn't a muscle car. But it was a start.

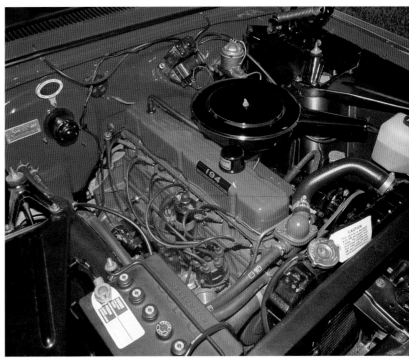

1964

Model availability	2-door sport coupe
Wheelbase	110 inches
Length	183 inches
Width	70.8 inches
Height	55 inches
Curb weight	2,675 pounds
Base price	$2,433
Track	56.8/56.3 (front/rear, in inches)
Wheels	14-inch
Tires	6.50 × 14 2-ply
Suspension	independent upper A-arms, lower controls arms, coil springs & stabilizer bar in front; solid axle w/single-leaf springs in back
Steering	recirculating ball (power-assist, optional)
Brakes	4-wheel drum
Engine	120-horsepower 194-cubic-inch inline 6-cyl., standard 155-horsepower 230-cubic-inch inline 6-cyl., optional 195-horsepower 283-cubic-inch V-8, optional
Bore & stroke	3.563 × 3.25 inches, 194 six; 3.875 × 3.25 inches, 230 six; 3.875 × 3.00 inches, 283 V-8
Compression	8.5:1, 6-cyl.; 9.25:1, 283 V-8
Fuel delivery	1-barrel carburetor, 6-cyl.; 2-barrel carburetor, 283 V-8
Transmission	3-speed manual, standard; 4-speed manual & Powerglide automatic, optional

Above left: Standard inside 1963's Nova SS were bucket seats, a deluxe steering wheel, and extra instrumentation.

Above right: The only engine offered beneath the 1963 Nova SS hood was a 194-cubic-inch six-cylinder rated at 120 horsepower.

Opposite: A convertible Nova Super Sport was offered for one year only, 1963. All others were sport coupes or sedans.

1964

Chevrolet management opted to drop the Nova sport coupe and convertible after 1963, despite healthy sales: nearly 87,500 for the closed model and 24,800 for its topless running mate. And with these two class acts' departures, so too went the Super Sport. For the moment.

Countering this bad news was the introduction of the Chevy II's first optional, factory-direct V-8, a 195-horsepower 283-cubic-inch small-block (RPO L32) that, according to *Motor Trend*'s Bob McVay, "takes the Chevy II out of the ho-hum category and makes it fun to drive." Acceleration wasn't mind-boggling, but speeding things up wasn't

that tough for enterprising owners considering all the hot small-block parts then available from Chevrolet. Swapping out the L32's two-barrel carburetor for the four-barrel crowning the new midsized Chevelle's 220-horsepower L77 283 was just a start. Truly inspired home mechanics also might have traded the 283 for the 327, which was making 300 horses in top form for both Chevelle and Chevy's full-sizers in 1964.

It was Chevelle's debut that reportedly influenced the decision to cut the Nova Super Sport loose after only one year on the market. Apparently some execs felt that leaving sport-minded Chevy II customers out in the cold might inspire them to move up to their all-new intermediate. But hot-headed compact buyers would have nothing of it. Their complaints forced Chevrolet to bring back the Nova sport coupe and SS early in the 1964 run, with the Super Sport now listed as the new flagship model series. The convertible, unfortunately, was never seen again.

A 283-CU.-IN. V8 NEVER FOUND A HAPPIER HOME—We slung a big 195-hp 283-cubic-inch V8* into the Chevy II Nova Sport Coupe and now you'd think it was born that way.

This is the same Chevy II that spent a couple of happy years building up a following as one of the most wholesome things since brown bread. The one down-to-earth American car you wouldn't mind bringing home to mother or showing off to your friends. And the last car in the world you'd ever accuse of being pretentious. In short, a regular darb.

Now, with that V8 up front, Chevy II spends most of its time doing impressions of performance types. Give it a 4-speed all-synchro shift* and it's very close to being just that. After all, it started out with certain advantages: taut suspension, trim size, no-nonsense construction.

Is this any way for a nice, quiet, sturdy, sensible, unpretentious car like Chevy II to behave? Strangely enough, yes. Despite its new vigor, it's still a nice, quiet, sturdy, sensible, unpretentious car. With sharper teeth. Grrr. **CHEVY II NOVA**   *CHEVROLET*

Chevrolet Division of General Motors, Detroit, Michigan   *Optional at extra cost

All features, including the standard 194-cubic-inch six, carried over for 1964's Super Sport. The only notable upgrades involved the deletion of the Nova's bodyside trim spear and the relocation of the Nova SS badges from the quarter panels to the front fenders. Chevrolet's bigger, better 230-cube six was optional, but who cared when the 283 V-8 also was waiting on the RPO list? Price for the L32 small-block was $107. A new and optional Muncie four-speed (priced at $188) also debuted for the warmly welcomed V-8.

Along with the 283 came bigger, hopefully better, brakes. Front drums went from 9 inches in diameter to 9.5 and from 2.25 inches wide to 2.5. Rear drums measured 9.5 × 2 inches, compared to the 9 × 1.75 units used previously. Clutch, transmission, and rear axle also were beefed, and all V-8 Chevy IIs received larger 14 × 5 wheels.

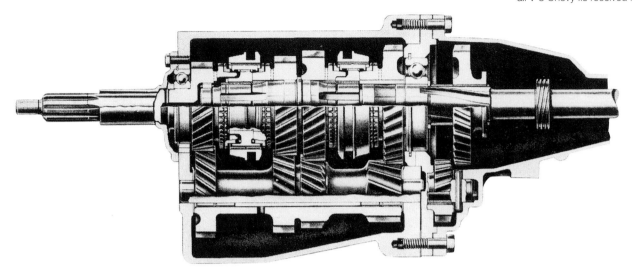

Left: Along with V-8 power, a Muncie four-speed manual transmission became optional for the Nova SS in 1964. *GM*

Opposite: Chevrolet was more than happy to announce the introduction of an optional factory-installed V-8 for 1964's Nova. *GM*

Below: After moving from the rear quarter panel to the front fender in 1964, the Nova SS script returned to the tail the following year. The strongest engine option for 1965's Nova SS was the L74 327 small-block, rated at 300 horsepower. *GM*

1965

Unchanged for four years, the Chevy II body looked old beyond its years compared to the fresh-faced Chevelle, not to mention Corvair and big Chevys, cars featuring markedly attractive total makeovers in 1965. Save for a new grille and more roaming badges ("Nova SS" returned to the rear quarters), next to nothing changed as far as the top-shelf Chevy II series was concerned—at least nothing in the image department.

But making really big news beneath the 1965 Super Sport's hood were even more power choices. Chevy officials even went so far as to segregate this year's SS models into two separate sub-series, specially coded for the six and V-8, to help keep things in order. The 194 six was again standard for the former, with the 230 six optional. The L32 283 two-barrel small-block was standard for the latter, joined midyear by the optional 220-horsepower L77, with its four-barrel carb and dual exhausts.

More notable were two optional 327s, both of which featured four-barrel carburetors and 10:1 compression. The L30 327 produced 250 horsepower, while its L74 brother made 300.

Opposite: This Nova SS features the 350-horsepower L79 327. Standard power that year again came from Chevy's 194-cubic-inch six-cylinder.

Below: Freshened styling enhanced Nova SS appeal in 1966, as did the optional L79 V-8, a 327-cubic-inch small-block first seen in Corvette ranks in 1965.

1965

Model availability	2-door sport coupe
Wheelbase	110 inches
Length	183 inches
Width	70.8 inches
Height	55 inches
Curb weight	2,690 pounds
Base price	$2,381
Track	56.8/56.3 (front/rear, in inches)
Wheels	14-inch stamped-steel
Tires	6.50 × 14 two-ply
Suspension	independent upper A-arms, lower controls arms, coil springs & stabilizer bar in front; solid axle w/single-leaf springs in back
Steering	recirculating ball (power-assist, optional)
Brakes	4-wheel drum
Engine	120-horsepower 194-cubic-inch inline 6-cylinder, standard
	140-horsepower 230-cubic-inch inline 6-cylinder, optional
	195-horsepower 283-cubic-inch V-8, optional
	220-horsepower 283-cubic-inch V-8, optional
	250-horsepower 327-cubic-inch V-8, optional
	300-horsepower 327-cubic-inch V-8, optional
Bore & stroke	3.563 × 3.25 inches, 194 six; 3.875 × 3.25 inches, 230 six; 3.875 × 3.00 inches, 283 V-8; 4.00 × 3.25 inches, 327 V-8
Compression	8.5:1, six-cylinder; 9.25:1, 283 V-8; 10:1, 327 V-8
Fuel delivery	1-barrel carburetor, 6-cylinder; 2-barrel carburetor, 195-horsepower 283 V-8; 4-barrel carburetor, 220-horsepower 283 and 327 V-8s
Transmission	3-speed manual, standard; 4-speed manual & Powerglide automatic, optional

1966

Model availability . . . . 2-door sport coupe
Wheelbase . . . . 110 inches
Length . . . . 183 inches
Width . . . . 71.3 inches
Height . . . . 53.8 inches
Curb weight 3,140 (w/V-8)
Base price $2,430
Track . . . . 56.8/56.3 (front/rear, in inches)
Wheels . . . . 14-inch stamped-steel
Suspension . . . . independent upper A-arms, lower controls arms, coil springs & stabilizer bar in front; solid axle w/single-leaf springs in back
Steering . . . . recirculating ball (power-assist, optional)
Brakes . . . . 4-wheel drum
Engine . . . . 120-horsepower 194-cubic-inch inline 6-cylinder, standard
140-horsepower 230-cubic-inch inline 6-cylinder, optional
195-horsepower 283-cubic-inch V-8, optional
220-horsepower 283-cubic-inch V-8, optional
275-horsepower 327-cubic-inch V-8, optional
350-horsepower 327-cubic-inch V-8, optional
Bore & stroke . . . . 3.563 × 3.25 inches, 194 six; 3.875 × 3.25 inches, 230 six; 3.875 × 3.00 inches, 283 V-8; 4.00 × 3.25 inches, 327 V-8
Compression 8.5:1, 6-cylinder; 9.25:1, 283 V-8; 10.25:1, 275-horsepower 327 V-8; 11:1, 350-horsepower 327 V-8
Fuel delivery . . . . 1-barrel carburetor, 6-cylinder; 2-barrel carburetor, 195-horsepower 283 V-8; 4-barrel carburetor, 220-horsepower 283 and 327 V-8s
Transmission . . . . 3-speed manual, std.; 4-speed manual & Powerglide automatic, optional

1966

A squeaky-clean restyle arrived this year, while basic structure and powertrain features rolled over. Modernized lines were crisp, and 1966's new semi-fastback shape fit right in with Detroit's latest fad. "Style-wise, the Nova SS isn't likely to win any design laurels, but neither is it a bad-looking car," wrote *Motor Trend*'s Steve Kelly in trivializing tribute. Overall, the latest body also looked bigger even though basic chassis dimensions didn't change.

The engine lineup also stayed the same—that is, until a buyer reached the optional 327 V-8s. The L30 327 went from 250 horsepower to 275 in 1966, while the 300-horsepower L74 was deleted in favor of the groundbreaking L79. Introduced for Corvettes in 1965, this seriously strong small-block relied on a Holley four-barrel on an aluminum intake, big-valve heads, and 11:1 compression to produce more than one horsepower per cubic inch—350 to be exact.

In the little Nova SS, those ponies helped create one of Detroit's greatest street sleepers of all time—who would have ever guessed a compact could be so big and bad? Rest to 60 miles per hour required only 7.2 seconds, according to a *Car Life* road test that also produced a 15.1-second quarter mile. Breaking into the 14s was simply a matter of replacing those skinny standard treads with some real meat out back.

The L79's appearance signaled a coming of age for the Nova Super Sport as it finally could claim full-fledged muscle car status. And at about $3,600, it also represented one of the biggest bangs for the buck in 1966. Its diminutive nature too was a plus, while its hydraulically cammed heart was both nasty and nice at the same time. "Unlike some samples from the Supercar spectrum, [the L79 Nova] maintains a gentleness along with its fierce performance potential; its power/weight ratio is second to none and it is definitely better balanced than most," concluded *Car Life*'s critics.

Right: Notice the opposed twin snorkels on the 1966 Nova's L79 327. In Chevelle applications, these intakes were angled diagonally toward the headlight areas.

Below: Strato-bucket seats were standard inside the 1966 Nova SS, as was a console for the optional four-speed or Powerglide automatic transmissions. Transmission choices behind the L79 V-8 numbered two: a close- or wide-ratio four-speed manual.

1967

The 1967 Super Sport Nova looked essentially identical to its predecessor, and with the L79 (down-rated to 325 horsepower this year) dropped early on, it was left to the 275-horsepower 327 to carry the load. Bam! Just like that, the Nova SS again found itself lost well back in Detroit's high-performance pack. The 195-horsepower 283 small-block carried over for one last year as the Nova's standard V-8, but the 220-horsepower L77 did not return. Other mechanical news of note came in the brake department, where a safety-conscious dual-circuit master cylinder became standard and optional front discs appeared for the first time. Included with those disc brakes were attractive 14-inch Rally wheels, soon to become Chevy muscle car trademarks.

Below: No notable exterior changes marked the arrival of the latest Nova SS in 1967. The same stacked script showed up on both 1966's and 1967's Super Sport Nova quarter panels.

1967

Model availability	2-door sport coupe
Wheelbase	110 inches
Length	183 inches
Width	71.3 inches
Height	53.8 inches
Curb weight	2,690 pounds (w/6-cylinder)
Base price	$2,467
Track	56.8/56.3 (front/rear, in inches)
Wheels	14-inch stamped-steel
Suspension	independent upper A-arms, lower controls arms, coil springs & stabilizer bar in front; solid axle w/single-leaf springs in back
Steering	recirculating ball (power-assist, optional)
Brakes	4-wheel drum, std.; front discs optional
Engine	120-horsepower 194-cubic-inch inline 6-cylinder, standard
	155-horsepower 250-cubic-inch inline 6-cylinder, optional
	195-horsepower 283-cubic-inch V-8, optional
	275-horsepower 327-cubic-inch V-8, optional
	325-horsepower 327-cubic-inch V-8, optional (very few released early in year)
Bore & stroke	3.563 × 3.25 inches, 194 six; 3.875 × 3.25 inches, 230 six; 3.875 × 3.00 inches, 283 V-8; 4.00 × 3.25 inches, 327 V-8
Compression	8.5:1, 6-cylinder; 9.25:1, 283 V-8; 10.25:1, 275-horsepower 327 V-8; 11:1, 325-horsepower 327 V-8
Fuel delivery	1-barrel carburetor, 6-cylinder; 2-barrel carburetor, 195-horsepower 283 V-8; 4-barrel carburetor, 327 V-8
Transmission	3-speed manual, std.; 4-speed manual & Powerglide automatic, optional

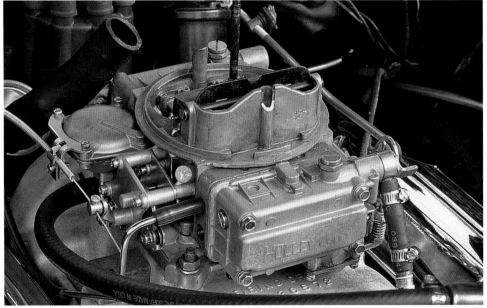

Above left: Optional front disc brakes debuted for 1967's Nova, and included with these stoppers was a set of attractive Rally wheels.

Above right: Only a handful of L79 installations were performed early in 1967 before the option was cancelled. Output this time around was 325 horsepower.

Right: The L79's Holley four-barrel was mounted on an aluminum intake in 1966 and 1967.

Opposite: A notably restyled Chevy II body debuted for 1968, and the Nova SS this year was fitted with a 350-cubic-inch small-block in base form.

1968

A second modernizing restyle appeared in 1968, but this time was supported by a nicely revamped unitized foundation that the latest Chevy II shared with its year-old Camaro cousin. Though curbside kibitzers liked to claim that the new Nova was little more than a Camaro in disguise, in truth it was the other way around. Engineers had this platform in the works already when Chevrolet's pony car project was kicked off; it was the Camaro that did the borrowing before appearing one year earlier than the updated Chevy II.

The bolt-on subframe design, front suspension, cowl structure, and mono plate rear springs more or less carried over between the two, as did standard staggered rear shock absorbers. Reserved for the Camaro's hotter optional V-8s in 1967, these shocks were bias mounted—the passenger-side unit in front of the axle, its opposite mate behind—to prevent dangerous wheel hop brought on during hard acceleration. All 1968 Novas fitted with optional engines also received stronger multi-leaf springs in back to further limit unwanted axle wind-up whenever pedal met metal.

Overall, 1968's Chevy II was longer, taller, and notably heavier than its forerunner. Wheelbase was stretched a click to 111 inches, while track went

1968

Model availability	2-door coupe
Wheelbase	111 inches
Length	187.7 inches
Width	70.5 inches
Height	54.1 inches
Curb weight	3,400 pounds (w/350 V-8)
Base price	$2,367 (V-8 2-door coupe), plus $210.65 for L48 SS package, $368.65 for L34, $500.30 for L78
Track	59/58.9 (front/rear, in inches)
Wheels	14 × 6
Tires	E70 × 14 Uniroyal Tiger Paw
Suspension	independent A-arms, heavy-duty coil springs & stabilizer bar in front; solid axle w/multi-leaf springs in back
Steering	recirculating ball (power-assist, optional)
Brakes	4-wheel drum
Engine	295-horsepower 350-cubic-inch L48 V-8, standard / 350-horsepower 396-cubic-inch L34 V-8, optional / 375-horsepower 396-cubic-inch L78 V-8, optional
Bore & stroke	4.00 × 3.25 inches, 350 V-8; 4.094 × 3.76 inches, 396 V-8
Compression	10.25:1, 350 V-8 and L34 396 V-8; 11:1, L78 396 V-8
Fuel delivery	4-barrel carburetor
Transmission	3-speed manual, standard; 4-speed manual & Powerglide automatic, optional

up markedly: from 56.8 inches to 59 in front, from 56.3 to 58.9 in back. Body style choices, on the other hand, were cut back to just two sedans—one with two doors, the other four—as the stylish sport coupe (not to mention the yeoman station wagon) joined its convertible ancestor in the archives, also never to return.

Notable too this year was the complete merging of nameplates as all models were simply called Chevy II Novas. Even the Super Sport wore Chevy II identification (above the grille) in 1968, something earlier renditions didn't in keeping with their elite image. With a topline Nova series no longer present, the body styles were now segregated rather plainly by engine choice: prefix code 111 for four-cylinder models, 113 for the sixes, and 114 for the V-8s. Body style codes were 69 for the four-door, 27 for the two-door.

Replacing the retired 283 as the Nova's standard V-8 in 1968 was Chevrolet's new 307-cubic-inch Turbo Fire engine, created by bolting a 327 crank into a 283 block. This mild-mannered motor was one of the few small-blocks to never see a high-performance transformation. Topped by a two-barrel carburetor, it produced a polite 200 horsepower.

More to leadfoots' liking was the optional L79 327, which apparently reappeared midyear in 1968. Again rated at 325 horsepower, this rather mysterious mill differed from earlier renditions in that it used a Quadrajet four-barrel carb (topped by a Corvette-style open-element air cleaner) on a cast-iron intake. But still a certified screamer, it was capable of blasting a 1968 Chevy II (with sticky slicks bolted on in back) through the quarter mile in 14.6 seconds, according to a *Hot Rod* magazine road test.

Hardly any L79 V-8s found their way into Novas in 1968, the last year for the 327 in Chevy II ranks. None were bolted into 1968 Super Sports as the latest SS at first was limited to one power source when it went on sale on September 21 that year. Sixes were no longer offered either as Chevrolet's 350-cubic-inch Turbo Fire small-block, introduced the previous year exclusively as a Camaro SS option, became standard fare for the car called "Chevy II much" in company advertisements. With no less than 295 horses now at the ready, the SS Nova was once more worthy of nomination to the muscle car class. "You'll second the motion," added those ads.

The latest in a long line of bulked-up small-blocks, the Camaro's 350 Turbo Fire wasn't simply the product of a little boring or stroking, as had been basically the case both when the original 265 morphed into the 283 in 1957 and the 283 evolved into the 327 five years later. Stretching the 265/283's 3.00-inch stroke to 3.25 inches was no big deal, and a little extra iron had to be cast into the cylinder walls to allow ample room for the 327's 4.00-inch bores. Job done.

To make 350 cubic inches, engineers combined the existing 4.00-inch bore with a new 3.48 stroke. And with more power potential present thanks to its added displacement, the 350 required some significant lower-end reinforcement to help hold

things together under duress. Beefier connecting rods and a tougher crank with enlarged journals were the most noticeable: 2.45 inches for the main bearings, 2.10 for the rods. Cranks journals for the 265/283/327 trio measured 2.30 inches (mains) and 2.00 (rods). Extra counterweights were required to balance the new crank, and that added material, working in concert with the heavier shaft's longer throws, meant that the 350's block had to be modified to allow ample room for everything to rotate. Extra webbing and thicker bulkheads also were cast into the block for added durability.

Even more support came in 1968. From 1955 to '67, all Chevy small-blocks relied on two-bolt caps to hold the crank's five main bearings in place. Beginning the next year, all high-performance small-blocks with 4.00-inch bores (save for the 327) received stronger four-bolt main caps for the three inner bearings. And these four-bolt blocks were recast with extra iron in their inner bulkheads to allow all those bolts to torque up tight.

No longer an individual model, 1968's Nova SS, like its Camaro counterpart, was created by checking off its exclusive engine code: RPO L48. Priced at $210.65, this package added 14 × 6 wheels wearing E70 redline rubber and a tidy collection of dress-up items: simulated air intakes on the hood, Super Sport block letters along the front fenders' lower edges, blacked-out grille and rear deck panel, and SS badges at both ends and on the steering wheel. The deal didn't include bucket seats, standard equipment on all earlier SS Novas, but they were optional, along with a console and gauge package.

The star of the show was the 295-horsepower 350, which brought along with it heavy-duty springs, radiator, and clutch, as well as a high-performance starter motor. A three-speed stick was standard behind the L48; options included a heavy-duty three-speed, close- (M21) or wide-ratio (M20) four-speeds, and the Powerglide automatic.

As attractive as this new Nova SS was, few buyers took note in 1968, and fewer got wind of an even meaner rendition released later that year. Just as the L48 small-block carried over from the Camaro, so too did the 396-cubic-inch Mk IV big-block, also introduced for the Super Sport pony car in 1967. First seen beneath Corvette, Chevelle, and full-sized Chevy hoods in 1965, the 396 Turbo Jet V-8 was offered in two forms for the 1968 Nova SS: the 350-horsepower L34 and 375-horsepower L78.

With a hydraulic cam and Rochester four-barrel carb, the L34 appeared rather tame in comparison to the L78, which used solid lifters and was fed by an 800-cfm Holley four-barrel. The heavy-duty M13 three-speed manual was standard behind both big-blocks. M20 and M21 Muncie four-speeds and the Powerglide or Turbo Hydra-Matic automatics were optional for the L34. No automatics were offered behind the brutal L78, but two top-shelf four-speeds were: the M21 and the super-heavy-duty M22 "Rock Crusher," nicknamed for its noisy, gnarly gears.

Talk about a sleeper. The new big-block Nova gave away its presence only by way of super-small 396 lettering included along with the side marker light on each front fender. Most unsuspecting stoplight challengers never knew what had hit them after a tangle with one of these very rare, totally unassuming beasts.

"All docile and innocent . . . the vestal virgin image pales slightly when you turn on the engine," went *Car and Driver*'s lead-in for its road test of a 375-horse 1968 Nova SS. Published performance stats were 5.9 seconds for the 0 to 60 run, 14.5 seconds at 101.1 miles per hour for the quarter mile.

1968 COPO

While official Chevrolet paperwork didn't list an available automatic transmission option for the L78 SS 396 Nova when it appeared in April 1968, fifty such packages were put together for Chevy dealer Fred Gibb using the clandestine COPO pipeline. COPO was short for Central Office Production Order, a special request procedure typically used by fleet buyers to circumvent corporate red tape. If a commercial vehicle customer desired an unlisted combination of off-the-shelf parts, a COPO represented just the ticket—it didn't require upper management approval, only a go-ahead from the guys in Engineering who would be handling the job.

COPOs came in especially handy for performance product guru Vince Piggins, whose job during the sixties was to promote Chevy performance any way he could despite various limitations imposed by corporate execs. Remember, Chevrolet wasn't supposed to

be in racing, per that infamous decree sent down from GM in 1963. Yet there was the competition-conscious Z28 Camaro dashing about SCCA tracks four years later. The Z28 was Piggins's baby, and so were the legendary COPO Camaros and Chevelles built in 1969 with Corvette-sourced 427-cubic-inch big-block V-8s—combinations that supposedly were taboo prior to 1970 per GM's 400-cube limit for V-8s going into its divisions' pony cars and midsized models.

Fast-thinking dealers like Fred Gibb became regular callers to Piggins's office a half-century back. Opened in LaHarpe, Illinois, in 1947, Gibb Chevrolet was home to various COPO creations, thanks to its owner's drag racing ventures, which began after his top salesman bought a Z28 in

Above: Dick Harrell also swapped Corvette 427s into Chevelles, Camaros, and Novas, and he marketed these conversions through a distribution network similar to Don Yenko's. This 427-powered 1968 Nova sports a Harrell trademark—a Corvette-style stinger hood scoop. *Tom Shaw*

Left: In 1968, Illinois Chevy dealer Fred Gibb (standing proudly here) noticed that drag racing's super-stock classes were devoid of capable auto-trans Chevrolets, thanks in part to the absence of an automatic option for the new 375-horsepower Nova SS. He then contacted Vince Piggins, who concocted COPO No. 9738, which added GM's Turbo Hydra-Matic 400 into the L78 Nova mix. Gibb Chevrolet raced one of these COPO Novas (also shown here), with Dick Harrell doing the driving. *Courtesy Bob McClurg*

Opposite: Vince Piggins was the main man behind various supposedly taboo Chevrolet performance projects during the sixties, including the Z28 Camaro. He also freely used the COPO paper trail to deliver Corvette-powered Chevelles and Camaros to dealers like Don Yenko in 1969. The COPO Novas of 1968 were his work as well.

1967 and started campaigning it as *Little Hoss*. In 1968, *Little Hoss* won an American Hot Rod Association stock-class world championship.

Early that summer, Gibb took note of the fact that drag racing's automatic-trans super-stock classes were strangely devoid of capable Chevys, thanks in part to the absence of an auto-box option for the new 375-horsepower SS Nova. He then contacted Piggins, who concocted COPO number 9738, which added Chevrolet's superior Turbo Hydra-Matic 400 automatic into the L78 Nova mix.

National Hot Rod Association rules required a minimum run of fifty cars to allow said models to legally compete in its stock classes, thus the logic behind Gibb Chevrolet's order. All fifty COPO 9738 Novas were built during the first two weeks of July 1968, and all featured the same equipment: joining the L78 396 and TH400 trans were a heavy-duty radiator, 4.10:1 Positraction differential, painted 14 × 6 steel wheels, power-assisted drum brakes, bucket seats, and floor shifter with console. The radio was deleted and two interior colors were specified, black or blue. Exterior finishes were Fathom Blue, Grecian Green, Matador Red, and Tripoli Turquoise. Gibb kept one COPO Nova to race himself and sold the rest—the price on his LaHarpe lot was $3,592.12.

The plot thickened further after some twenty or so COPO 9738 cars ended up in the hands of veteran drag racer Dick Harrell, who operated a Chevrolet dealership network based out of Kansas City, Missouri. Known as Mr. Chevrolet, Harrell was AHRA Driver of the Year in 1969, and he also was responsible for helping develop 427 Camaro conversions for both Yenko Chevrolet in Pennsylvania and Nickey Chevrolet in Chicago. Harrell applied this same approach to the COPO Novas he acquired, trading the L78s for 450-horsepower 427s backed by competition-prepped automatics. Additional equipment varied, with some featuring Jardine headers, Chevy Rally wheels, M&H slicks, traction bars, and fiberglass hoods with Corvette-style "stinger" scoops. Cragar mags too appeared. The typical price for a Harrell Nova was about $4,400.

Yenko Chevrolet, Nickey Chevrolet, and Baldwin/Motion Performance all also offered 427 Novas, with Baldwin/Motion later making truly wild 454 big-block swaps too. Unlike Yenko's Super Car Chevelles and Camaros, which began life in 1969 as factory-equipped 427 COPO models, its S/C Nova that year was a swap job performed in the Pennsylvania dealership's shop.

1969

Only the Nova name carried over from 1968 as the painfully plain Chevy II tag finally fell by the wayside at year's end. Simulated louvers added to the front fenders represented the most notable exterior update to 1969's Super Sport package, now listed under RPO Z26. New beneath the skin were standard front disc brakes, which didn't necessarily guarantee the installation of Rally wheels as in

1968 COPO 9738

Model availability	2-door coupe
Wheelbase	111 inches
Length	187.7 inches
Width	70.5 inches
Height	54.1 inches
Price	$3,591.12 (on Gibb Chevrolet lot in LaHarpe, Illinois)
Track	59/58.9 (front/rear, in inches)
Wheels	14 × 6 stamped-steel
Tires	Firestone E70 Wide Ovals
Suspension	independent A- arms, heavy-duty coil springs & stabilizer bar in front; solid axle w/multi-leaf springs in back
Steering	recirculating ball
Brakes	4-wheel drums w/power-assist
Engine	375-horsepower 396-cubic-inch L78 V-8 (some converted to 427 V-8s by Chevy dealer Dick Harrell)
Bore & stroke	4.094 × 3.76 inches
Compression	11:1
Fuel delivery	4-barrel carburetor
Transmission	Turbo Hydra-Matic 400 automatic
Rear axle	4.10:1 Positraction

Above: A blacked-out grille was again standard for Nova SS in 1969. This model is one of 5,262 Super Sports built that year with the 375-horsepower L78 396 Turbo Jet.

Opposite: The 375-horsepower L78 396 was available for Chevelle, Camaro, and Nova Super Sports in 1969. L78 highlights included an 800-cfm Holley four-barrel, solid lifters, and 11:1 compression.

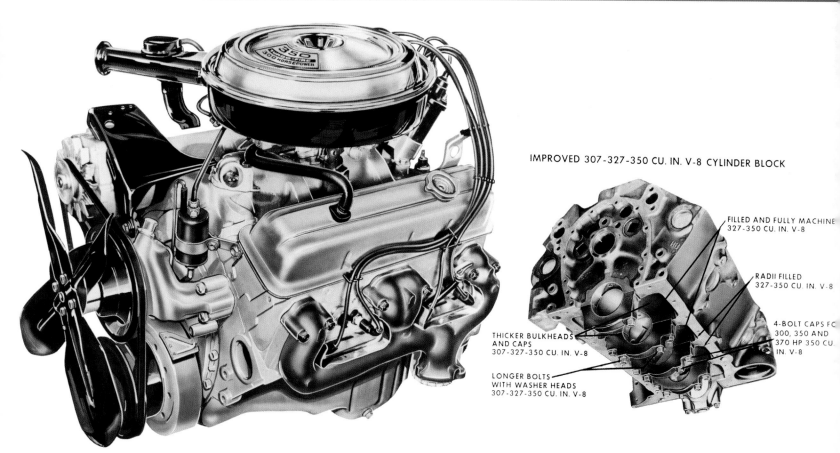

IMPROVED 307-327-350 CU. IN. V-8 CYLINDER BLOCK

FILLED AND FULLY MACHINE
327-350 CU. IN. V-8

RADII FILLED
327-350 CU. IN. V-8

4-BOLT CAPS FC
300, 350 AND
370 HP 350 CU.
IN. V-8

THICKER BULKHEADS
AND CAPS
307-327-350 CU. IN. V-8

LONGER BOLTS
WITH WASHER HEADS
307-327-350 CU. IN. V-8

Above left: The Nova Super Sport's base small-block, the L48 350 V-8, was bumped up to 300 horsepower in 1969 and stayed at that level for 1970. *GM*

Above right: By 1970, the Mouse Motor's cylinder block was as tough as it got thanks to various upgrades made since 1967. Most notable were the four-bolt main bearing caps applied in 1968. *GM*

Opposite top: Unlike its 427-equipped Camaro/Chevelle Super Cars, which began life as COPO models, Yenko Chevrolet's Corvette-powered Nova was the product of a swap job in 1969. *Tom Shaw*

Opposite bottom: Like its 396-cube sibling, Chevrolet's 427 Turbo Jet big-block nestled nicely into the Nova engine compartment in 1969. But even Don Yenko himself admitted that maybe this brutal combo wasn't one of his better ideas. *Tom Shaw*

the past. Joining those Rally rims on 1969's options list were the same 14 × 7 five-spoke sport wheels seen on that year's Camaro and Chevelle Super Sports.

New too were various optional Turbo Hydra-Matic automatic transmissions. The TH 350 automatic was offered behind the standard 350 small-block, boosted this year to 300 horsepower. The TH400 was available behind the 350-horsepower 396, and a specially equipped version of this transmission was listed for the top-dog L78 big-block.

1969

SS

Model availability	2-door coupe
Wheelbase	111 inches
Length	187.7 inches
Width	70.5 inches
Height	54.1 inches
Weight	3,373 pounds (SS 396)
Base price	RPO Z26 SS package (w/350 V-8) cost $280.20; L34 V-8 added another $184.35; L78 added $316
Track	59/58.9 (front/rear, in inches)
Wheels	14 × 7
Tires	E70 × 14 Uniroyal Tiger Paw
Suspension	independent A-arms, heavy-duty coil springs & stabilizer bar in front; solid axle w/multi-leaf springs in back
Steering	recirculating ball (power-assist, optional)
Brakes	front discs, rear drums
Engine	300-horsepower 350-cubic-inch L48 V-8, standard 350-horsepower 396-cubic-inch L34 V-8, optional 375-horsepower 396-cubic-inch L78 V-8, optional (L89 aluminum heads, optional)
Bore & stroke	4.00 × 3.25 inches, 350 V-8; 4.094 × 3.76 inches, 396 V-8
Compression	10.25:1, 350 V-8 & L34 396 V-8; 11:1, L78 396 V-8
Fuel delivery	4-barrel carburetor
Transmission	3-speed manual, standard; 4-speed manual, Powerglide, TH350 & TH400 automatics, optional **Note:** 396 Turbo Jet V-8 was bored out to 402 cubic inches late in 1969.

1970

Model availability	2-door coupe
Wheelbase	111 inches
Length	187.7 inches
Width	70.5 inches
Height	54.1 inches
Weight	3,515 pounds (w/350 V-8)
Base price	$2,793 (w/350 V-8)
Track	59/58.9 (front/rear, in inches)
Wheels	14 × 7
Tires	E70 × 14 Uniroyal Tiger Paw
Suspension	independent A-arms, heavy-duty coil springs & stabilizer bar in front; solid axle w/multi-leaf springs in back
Steering	recirculating ball (power-assist, optional)
Brakes	front discs, rear drums
Engine	300-horsepower L48 350-cubic-inch V-8, standard
	350-horsepower L34 402-cubic-inch V-8, optional
	375-horsepower L78 402-cubic-inch V-8, optional
Bore & stroke	4.00 × 3.25 inches, 350 V-8; 4.126 × 3.76 inches, 402 V-8
Compression	10.25:1, 350 V-8 and 350-horsepower 402 V-8; 11:1, 375-horsepower 402 V-8
Fuel delivery	4-barrel carburetor
Transmission	3-speed manual, standard; 4-speed manual, Powerglide, TH350 & TH400 automatics, optional

1970

Revised taillights and a new grille represented the easiest way to identify a 1970 Nova SS. Beneath the hood, Chevy's latest Mk IV big-block was bored out slightly from 4.094 inches to 4.126, upping the cubic inch count to 402. All labels, however, still read "396 Turbo Jet." Why displace the boat, right?

The 300-horsepower L48 small-block remained the base V-8 for 1970's Super Sport, and the two 402-cube big-blocks still produced 350 and 375 horses, respectively. Unfortunately this was the last year for the L34 and L78 in Nova SS ranks as Chevrolet's compact performance legacy began its final downturn.

Opposite top: Revised taillights set 1970's Nova apart from its forerunners. A new grille also appeared up front. *GM*

Opposite bottom: The SS 396 Nova made one final appearance in 1970. Two big-blocks remained available that year: the 350-horsepower L34 and 375-horsepower L78. *GM*

Below: Yenko Chevrolet came back in 1970 with its small-block Yenko Deuce, a far easier sell than 1969's 427 Nova, which proved nearly impossible to insure. *Bob McClurg*

1970 YENKO DEUCE

Model availability	2-door coupe
Wheelbase	111 inches
Length	187.7 inches
Width	70.5 inches
Height	54.1 inches
Weight	3,515 pounds
Base price	$4,395
Track	59/58.9 (front/rear, in inches)
Wheels	14 × 7 SS five-spokes
Tires	E70 × 14 Uniroyal Tiger Paw
Suspension	independent A-arms, heavy-duty coil springs & stabilizer bar in front; solid axle w/multi-leaf springs in back
Steering	recirculating ball (power-assist, optional)
Brakes	power-assisted front discs, rear drums
Engine	360-horsepower 350-cubic-inch LT-1 V-8
Bore & stroke	4.00 × 3.25 inches
Compression	11:1
Fuel delivery	4-barrel carburetor
Transmission	close-ratio 4-speed manual, standard; TH350 automatic, optional
Rear axle	4.10:1 Positraction

1970 Yenko Deuce

Don Yenko's Chevy dealership in Canonsburg, Pennsylvania, planted only a few dozen 427 big-blocks into SS 396 Nova bodies in 1969, basically because the combo was just too nasty for public consumption. Stuffing 450 horses beneath those compact hoods translated into some seriously surreal performance, like rest to 60 miles per hour in something like four seconds. Even Yenko himself later called his 427 Nova "a real beast." "It was almost lethal," he added. "In retrospect, this probably wasn't the safest car in the world."

So Yenko Chevrolet came back in 1970 with a less-explosive Nova. Soaring insurance costs had transformed his S/C Chevelles and Camaros from tough sells into nearly impossible transactions, leaving him little choice but to send these two mean machines into the archives. In their place came the small-block Yenko Deuce, a 350-equipped Nova created through yet another COPO, this one coded number 9010.

A COPO was required because the 350 V-8 in this case wasn't offered for the 1970 Nova. Standard that year for the revamped Z28, optional for Corvette, was the hottest small-block yet, the solid-lifter LT-1, rated at 370 horsepower for the latter, 360 for the former. The COPO 9010 deal transplanted the 360-horsepower LT-1 350 into brown-paper-wrapper Novas, not Super Sports, but Yenko made up for the missing imagery by adding his own trademark graphics. Additional standard features included an M21 four-speed and 4.10 Posi gears. A Hurst shifter, power front discs, five-spoke SS wheels, and a hood-mounted tach were listed as standard options. The Turbo Hydra-Matic automatic transmission also was available.

A typical Yenko Deuce started at $4,395, not a bad price considering how little it cost to operate in dangerous daily traffic. As Yenko later explained, "Insurance companies wouldn't insure a 427 Camaro, but a 350 Nova was a normal family car. All the customer had to tell his agent was that the car was a 350 Nova. It was none of the agent's concern that the 350 was the solid-lifter LT-1 Corvette motor. We built two hundred of these cars and never heard a peep from the insurance companies."

In truth, the actual count was a bit lower. Chevrolet reportedly released 178 COPO 9010 Novas in 1970, with 176 going to Yenko Chevrolet. The other two were delivered to Central Chevrolet, in London, Ontario, thanks to salesman Dave Mathers, who originally ordered ten of these rather plain-looking certified muscle cars.

Left: The heart of the Yenko Deuce was the Corvette's LT-1 350, rated at 370 horsepower between fiberglass fenders in 1970. That year's Z28 Camaro also came standard with the LT-1, in this case rated at 360 horsepower. *GM*

For the 1970 Corvette, the LT-1 small-block was rated at 370 horsepower. Chevrolet's new Camaro Z28 that year was fitted with a 360-horse version of this solid-lifter V-8, and this rendition also found its way between Yenko Nova fenders. *Steve Statham*

1971

The fake fender louvers seen in 1969 and 1970 disappeared in 1971, and the same could be said about much of the SS Nova's performance abilities. Only one engine remained, the L48 small-block, now rated at 270 horsepower thanks mostly to a compression cut from 10.25:1 to 8.5:1. Though still no slouch, the L48 Nova certainly couldn't fill the treads of the retired SS 396. Gone too were heavy-duty front springs and the bright engine dress-up seen on previous SS V-8s. Optional transmission choices were limited to two: the wide-ratio M20 four-speed or Turbo 350 automatic.

Basically the same 350-powered SS Nova carried over into 1972 wearing a net-rated output tag of 200 horsepower. In 1973 an available six-cylinder returned to the Z26 package, then the last of the breed came and went rather meekly three years later.

1971

Model availability	2-door coupe
Wheelbase	111 inches
Length	187.7 inches
Width	70.5 inches
Height	54.1 inches
Weight	2,919 pounds
Base price	RPO Z26 cost $327.55
Track	59/58.9 (front/rear, in inches)
Wheels	14 × 7
Tires	E70 × 14 Uniroyal Tiger Paw
Suspension	independent upper A-arms, coil springs & stabilizer bar in front; solid axle w/multi-leaf springs in back
Steering	recirculating ball
Brakes	front discs, rear drums
Engine	270-horsepower 350-cubic-inch V-8
Bore & stroke	4.00 × 3.25 inches
Compression	8.5:1
Fuel delivery	4-barrel carburetor
Transmission	3-speed manual, standard; 4-speed manual & TH350 automatic, optional

Right: A compression cut helped drop the SS Nova's L48 350 to 270 horsepower in 1971. *GM*

Opposite top: Chevrolet introduced two low-buck fun machines in 1971, the Heavy Chevy Chevelle and Rally Nova. In base form, both offered a decent dose of performance at a lower price compared to their Super Sport counterparts. *GM*

Opposite bottom: Small-block power was the only choice for 1971's Nova SS.

1963–1971 Nova Super Sport Production Figures

Year	6-cylinder	V-8		Line Total
1963 (sport coupe & convertible)				42,432
1964 (sport coupe only)				10,576
1965 (sport coupe only)				9,100
1966 (sport coupe only)	**6-cylinder**	**V-8**		
	16,311	4,675		20,986[1]
	[1]included 3,547 L79 327 V-8s; total 1966 Chevy II L79 production, SS or not: 5,481			
1967 (sport coupe only)	8,213	1,856		10,069[2]
	[2]total 1967 Chevy II L79 production, SS or not: 6			
1968 (coupe only)	**L48 350**	**L34 396**	**L78 396**	
	4,670	234	667	5,571
	total 1968 Chevy II L79 production (non-SS); 1,274			
1969 (coupe only)	10,355	1,947	5,262[3]	17,654
	[3]included 311 w/L89 aluminum-head option			
1970 (coupe only)	14,021	1,802	3,765	19,588
1971 (coupe only)	7,015	n/a	n/a	7,015
	1971 Rally Nova production: 7,700			

NOTE: 396 Turbo Jet V-8 was bored out to 402 cubic inches late in 1969.

03

MIDSIZED
SUPER SPORTS

Chevelle, El Camino & Monte Carlo: 1964–1973

Chevrolet offered two definitely distinct model lines in 1959, with its familiar full-sized passenger-car group complemented by the Corvette, introduced six years prior. Corvair made it three in 1960, and 1962's Chevy II upped the ante to four, presumably the limit in the minds of some GM execs. But a notable gap existed, in both size and price, between the close-quartered Nova and the big Biscayne. Hence the decision to add a fifth model for 1964: Chevelle. Based on GM's new A-body platform, this midsizer also emerged to compete with Detroit's intermediate pioneer, Ford's Fairlane, unveiled for 1962.

- Bunkie Knudsen left Pontiac in November 1961 to take over Chevrolet's general manager post.
- Knudsen introduced the all-new Chevelle to the press in August 1963.
- Last seen in 1960, El Camino returned in downsized A-body form in 1964.
- Chevy's first SS 396 appeared in limited-edition form midyear in 1965.
- An SS 396 El Camino appeared in 1968.
- John DeLorean moved over from Pontiac to become Chevrolet general manager in March 1969, replacing another former Pontiac man, Pete Estes.
- The SS 396 Chevelle unseated Pontiac's GTO atop Detroit's muscle car sales leader board in 1969.
- Though its standard engine was bored out to 402 cubic inches late in 1969, the model name remained SS 396.
- SS 396 gear was available in the base 300 series for one year only, 1969.
- The SS 454 joined the SS 396 for 1970.
- The awesome LS6 V-8 was offered only for the Chevelle SS 454 in 1970, only for the Corvette in 1971.
- Small-block V-8s returned for Super Sport Chevelles in 1971.

Above: The original muscle car era's early sales leader, Pontiac's GTO, was unseated in 1969 by Chevrolet's SS 396 Chevelle, shown here celebrating with some smoky fireworks. *Tom Shaw*

Previous pages: Left: A blacked-out grille and twin hood bulges were included in 1966's SS 396 Chevelle deal. Some models apparently also featured blacked-out rear coves. The mag-style wheel covers seen here were optional; plain-Jane dog-dish hubcaps were standard. *Right:* Initial plans called for moving the existing Nova nameplate up into GM's new intermediate A-body ranks for 1964. A-body prototypes were still seen wearing Chevy II Nova identification as late as January 1963. *GM*

Opposite: Chevrolet general manager Semon E. "Bunkie" Knudsen introduced the all-new Chevelle to the press in August 1963. Raves quickly followed. *GM*

Formed more or less in clay by March 1962, Chevrolet's A-body image took on various identities before final transformation into sheet metal. Another clay seen a month later resembled an upsized Chevy II, and a mockup photographed in January 1963 even carried Chevy II Nova identification. "Indications are very strong that Chevrolet will modify the current Chevy II, making it wider and longer," predicted an August 1963 *Motor Trend* review. Mentioned too was the claim that the new model "might get a new name in the bargain."

Indeed, initial plans called for trading the Chevy II for the new A-body intermediate, with the thinking being another model line would surely eat into the division's proven four-tiered sales structure. Such worries, however, quickly faded, and the decision was made in February 1963 to put a fifth choice on the menu. The Nova didn't burn out, and one month later the Malibu moniker made its first appearance on an A-body mockup. But, like the Nova badge, this tag too represented icing on the cake. Per tradition, the true model name had to begin with a "C."

General manager Bunkie Knudsen introduced Chevelle to the press in August 1963. "Impressed by its clean and handsome styling, Detroit's normally undemonstrative auto reporters broke into spontaneous applause," announced a *Time*

magazine report. "The only complaint about the Chevelle was that dealers couldn't get enough of them," added *Automotive News* in September.

Within three months, Chevelle was the second hottest-selling Chevy, taking up 18 percent of the company's production schedule. When the smoke cleared, the final count for the 1964 Chevelle (discounting its second-generation El Camino derivative) totaled 354,571, tops in the intermediate ranks and some 75,000 greater than that year's Fairlane tally.

Along with that El Camino rendition (marketed as a truck), the Chevelle line included the base 300 series (available in two- and four-door sedan and two- and four-door station wagon forms) and the upscale Malibu, offered as a four-door sedan, two-door sport coupe, or convertible, and two- or four-door station wagon. Extra trim and more standard equipment typically set the top-shelf Malibu apart from the plain-Jane Chevelle 300, and both series featured six-cylinder and V-8 lines. All models rolled on a 115-inch wheelbase and featured coil springs at all four corners.

Chevy's A-body platform was revised for 1968, with a new 112-inch wheelbase created for two-doors, 116 inches for four-doors, station wagons, and El Caminos. Two years later Chevrolet introduced its classy Monte Carlo, a Chevelle-based two-door coupe that used the longer

116-inch wheelbase. Those 4 extra inches went into the Monte Carlo body ahead of the cowl, translating into the lengthiest hood in Chevrolet history. An SS454 version of this long-nosed coupe was offered for both 1970 and 1971.

1964

Nearly 23 percent of Chevelle's class-leading sales total in 1964 consisted of sexy Super Sports, available in Malibu hardtop or convertible forms. Both six-holers and V-8s were available for Chevy's first midsized SS, with base models featuring a 120-horsepower 194-cubic-inch straight-six. A 155-horsepower 230-cubic-inch six was optional. The base V-8 was a 195-horsepower 283-cubic-inch small-block fed by a two-barrel carb. Bucket seats were standard, as were a four-gauge instrument cluster (in place of the base model's idiot lights), a console with floorshift for Powerglide and four-speed models, and SS wheel covers.

Popular extra-cost items included Chevrolet's new Muncie four-speed gearbox, metallic brake linings, heavy-duty suspension and clutch, a tachometer in place of the clock (which moved to a pod on the dash), a Positraction differential, and 3.36:1 rear gears (3.08:1 cogs were standard). The strongest underhood option early on was RPO L77, a 220-horsepower 283 topped by a Rochester four-barrel. Then came an announcement in December 1963 that Chevrolet's 327-cubic-inch V-8 would be available between Chevelle fenders. Two were mentioned initially, the 250-horsepower L30 and its 300-horsepower L74 running mate, with the former debuting in March, the latter three months later.

Also debuting was the Corvette's smokin' L76 small-block, a 365-horsepower 327 that featured 11:1 compression and an aggressive solid-lifter cam. An L76 Chevelle was first mentioned in assembly manuals in late January 1964, and at least one prototype was built, a road rocket that apparently could hold its own with any muscle machine then running. According to *Motor Trend* spies, "the 325-horsepower GTO and 365-horsepower Chevelle are very comparable in performance, giving 0–60 times of around six seconds flat. They're far and away the hottest of the [new intermediates] and quicker than most big cars with high-performance engines."

Full production of the 365-horse Chevelle, however, never got rolling. Why? For various reasons, not the least of which was a shortage of 327s that developed early in 1964 due to unexpected demand from full-sized buyers. But, according to *Motor Trend*, "the biggest problem is that special exhaust manifolds are needed to clear the suspension in the Chevelle chassis." Apparently engineers wanted larger, better-flowing manifolds for the 300- and 365-horsepower applications, but none were ever cast. Relying on existing exhausts for the L74 clearly wasn't a problem; not so for the L76, which was killed off before it was born. According to a March 19 product update memo sent to the Chevrolet dealers, the 365-horse Turbo Fire 327 had "been cancelled and will not be offered" to Chevelle customers for 1964. Nonetheless, a few did fall into public hands.

1964 SS

Model availability	2-door Malibu hardtop/convertible (w/6-cylinder or V-8)
Wheelbase	115 inches
Length	193.9 inches
Width	74.6 inches
Height	54 inches
Curb weight	3,025 pounds (6-cylinder hardtop); 3,155 pounds (V-8 hardtop)
Base price	$2,538 (6-cylinder hardtop), $2,749 (6-cylinder convertible), $2,646 (V-8 hardtop), $2,857 (V-8 convertible)
Track	58 (front & rear, in inches)
Wheels	14-inch stamped-steel
Tires	6.50 × 14
Suspension	independent arms, coil springs & stabilizer bar in front; solid axle, upper/lower trailing arms, & coil springs in back
Steering	recirculating ball
Brakes	4-wheel drums
Transmission	3-speed manual, standard; 4-speed & Powerglide automatic, optional

Bucket seats were standard inside 1964's midsized Super Sport, as was a console for Powerglide or four-speed models.

Left: The Corvette's 365-horsepower L76 327 was briefly offered as a Malibu SS option early in 1964. Only a few L76 Super Sports were built before this clandestine package was cancelled.

Opposite: The Chevelle lineup was split up into six-cylinder and V-8 variations in 1964. The base V-8 was Chevrolet's 283-cubic-inch small-block, rated at 195 horsepower. *GM*

Right: Also borrowed from the Corvette, the L79 327 featured big-valve heads, 11:1 compression, and a Holley four-barrel carburetor. Output was 350 horsepower.

Opposite top: Restyled SS wheel covers appeared for 1965. New too was engine displacement identification for the front fender's cross-flag emblems. This SS convertible is powered by the base 283 small-block.

Opposite bottom: This 1965 El Camino is powered by that year's hottest available small-block, the L79 327.

Below: Introduced in 1959, Chevrolet's El Camino was dropped after 1960. It then returned as part of the Chevelle family in 1964, sharing all options, including powertrains. Super Sport features, however, did not carry over. G*M*

1965 SS

Model availability	2-door Malibu hardtop/convertible (w/6-cylinder or V-8)
Wheelbase	115 inches
Length	196.6 inches
Width	74.6 inches
Height	52.8 inches (hardtop)
Base price	$2,539 (6-cylinder hardtop), $2,750 (6-cylinder convertible), $2,647 (V-8 hardtop), $2,858 (V-8 convertible)
Track	58 (front/rear, in inches)
Wheels	14-inch stamped-steel
Tires	6.95 × 14
Suspension	independent A-arms, coil springs & stabilizer bar in front; solid axle, upper/lower trailing arms, & coil springs in back
Steering	recirculating ball
Brakes	4-wheel drums
Transmission	3-speed manual, standard; 4-speed & Powerglide automatic, optional

1965

A cleaner grille and larger taillights made up for the most noticeable appearance changes for 1965. Also present was a new wraparound bumper with a more pronounced point that helped add 2.5 inches to total length. Chassis refinements also lowered the car nearly an inch, making for a more rakish profile.

Malibu SS carried on in similar fashion, still equipped with a thrifty six-cylinder in base form.

The 195-horsepower 283 remained the base V-8, while the optional L77 283 was replaced by the 250-horsepower L30 327, at least initially. Although some factory literature indicated the L77 returned in February 1965, none showed up in that year's production records. The top performance option in the fall of 1964 was the 300-horsepower L74 327 with its big aluminum four-barrel, 10.5:1 compression, and dual exhausts.

An even hotter 327 made its way, again from Corvette ranks, onto the Chevelle options list not long after the 1965 models appeared. One of Chevrolet's strongest carbureted small-blocks, this L79 V-8 relied on a Holley four-barrel, big-valve heads, and 11:1 compression to help make 350 horsepower, and this with polite hydraulic lifters. "It's hard to believe Chevy's out of racing," claimed *Cars* magazine's Gordon Chittenden after roasting the rear tires on an L79 Chevelle.

1965 SS 396

Though certainly hot, the L79 Chevelle still was no match for Pontiac's GTO. Enter Vince Piggins, the former Hudson racing man then hawking horsepower at GM's entry-level division. In April 1963, he proposed dropping a 396-cubic-inch derivative of the legendary Mystery Motor into Chevy's upcoming A-body. But various glitches delayed development of this package. As it was, GM already had put a displacement limit (that translated into 330 cubes) on its new midsize models, making Piggins's proposal taboo.

Then Pontiac just had to go and boil things over with its 389-cubic-inch GTO. Chagrined GM execs had no choice but to raise that limit to 400 inches, in turn making a 396 Chevelle perfectly acceptable. Introduced in February 1965, this package was listed under RPO Z16 on factory paperwork. On the street the name soon was simply SS 396.

Beneath the first SS 396's hood was the Turbo Jet Mk IV big-block, a hydraulic-lifter V-8 rated at 375 horsepower for the A-body application. Behind it went a heavy-duty 11-inch clutch and a Muncie four-speed. No automatic was available. Additional special equipment included a high-torque starter, 61-ampere battery, five-blade thermo-modulated viscous-drive fan, large-capacity radiator with fan shroud, dual-snorkel air cleaner, and appropriate chrome dress-up.

1965 SS 396 (Z16)

Model availability	2-door Malibu hardtop/convertible
Wheelbase	115 inches
Length	196.6 inches
Width	74.6 inches
Height	52.8 inches
Shipping weight	3,565 pounds
Base price	RPO Z16 cost $1,501
Track	58 (front/rear, in inches)
Wheels	14 × 6 stamped-steel fitted w/mag-style deluxe wheel covers
Tires	7.74 × 14 gold-stripe
Suspension	independent A-arms, heavy-duty coil springs & stabilizer bar in front; solid axle, upper/lower trailing arms, heavy-duty coil springs & stabilizer bar in back
Steering	power-assisted recirculating ball (15.0:1 ratio)
Brakes	power-assisted 11-inch drums, front & rear
Transmission	4-speed manual

Only two hundred Z16 Malibu SS 396 hardtops, plus one clandestine convertible, were built in 1965, all fully loaded, and all wearing a price tag fit for a king. Standard features included mag-style wheel covers, power brakes and steering, heavy-duty suspension with stabilizer bars front and rear, 7.75 × 14 gold-stripe high-speed tires on 6-inch-wide wheels, padded dash with a clock mounted on top, 6,000-rpm tach, and Chevrolet's new AM/FM Multiplex stereo radio with four speakers. The total bill for RPO Z16 was $1,501.05. Add that to the $2,600 base price for a V-8 Malibu SS in 1965, and you get the picture. Most Z16s went to celebrities and prominent press people, all in the interest of kicking off a high-powered bloodline with a high-profile bang.

1966 SS 396

A restyled Chevelle with a mildly stated Coke-bottle body and trendy recessed rear window appeared for 1966, and the Malibu-based SS 396 returned as an individual model series all its own. No more sixes or small-blocks for the Super Sport Chevelle, it was big-block or no block at all for this midsized muscle car up until 1971.

More palatable base pricing also arrived in 1966, with an SS 396 hardtop starting at $2,776, its convertible running mate at $2,962. Cutting costs was simply a matter of also cutting both standard power and standard features. The idea, of course, was to widen the SS 396's appeal by putting it down within the reach of Average Joes everywhere. The plan worked gloriously as production soared to 72,272 for 1966.

In place of the Z16's 375-horsepower L37 396 was a more civilized standard Mk IV big-block, the 325-horsepower 396, listed as RPO L35 for El Camino applications. Gone from the standard package were the rigid convertible frame, big 11-inch full-sized Chevy brakes, and rear stabilizer bar. A three-speed manual was now the base

1966 SS 396

Model availability	2-door Malibu hardtop/convertible
Wheelbase	115 inches
Length	197 inches
Width	75 inches
Height	51.9 inches (hardtop), 52.8 inches (convertible)
Curb weight	3,800 pounds (hardtop)
Base price	$2,776 (hardtop), $2,962 (convertible)
Track	58 (front/rear, in inches)
Wheels	14 × 6 stamped-steel
Tires	7.75 × 14
Suspension	independent A-arms, coil springs & stabilizer bar in front; solid axle, upper/lower trailing arms, & coil springs in back
Steering	recirculating ball
Brakes	4-wheel drums
Transmission	3-speed manual, standard; 4-speed & Powerglide automatic, optional

Opposite: Gold-stripe tires and a blacked-out rear cove panel were just a few of the many standard features included as part of Chevrolet's first SS 396 deal, tagged RPO Z16, in 1965. Z16 production that year was 200 hardtops and one mysterious convertible.

Below: A convertible SS 396 officially appeared in the mainstream for 1966. Production was 5,429, compared to one for 1965.

transmission, and features such as the Z16's tach, fake mag wheel covers, and bucket seats became extra-cost options. No more standard Multiplex stereo either.

Appropriate badges in a blacked-out grille and on the rear cove panel, "Super Sport" rear-quarter script, and those legendary "396 Turbo Jet" cross-flags on each front fender identified the latest big-block Chevelle in 1966. So, too, did a

pair of hood bulges trimmed with nonfunctional grilles. Early brochures also showed a blacked-out rear cove, but apparently few models received this treatment. Color-accented rocker and lower rear-quarter moldings, wheel-opening trim, 7.75 × 14 redline tires on 6-inch rims, and small dog-dish hubcaps completed the deal.

If Z16-type performance was the goal, the options list was the place to shop. The Muncie

four-speed was there, as were special suspension components, a Positraction differential, and the L34 396, a 360-horse improvement on the L35. Both relied on 10.25:1 compression, while the hotter L34 used a lumpier cam and Holley four-barrel and was based on a beefier four-bolt block.

On the top shelf was the L78 396 Turbo Jet, rated at a familiar 375 horsepower. Making the L78 a force to be reckoned with were big-valve 427 heads, 11:1

Above: This cowl-induction air cleaner setup was a rare dealer option for 1966's SS 396 Chevelle.

Right: El Caminos, of course, wore different taillights than their passenger-car cousins due to the presence of that tailgate. Total 1966 production was 35,119—9,321 base models and 25,798 Custom El Caminos. *GM*

Opposite: Badges abounded on the 1967 Super Sport. If the stacked grille badges and model name on the front weren't enough, the front fender crossed-flags badge let everyone know what was hidden under the hood. *GM*

compression, and an aluminum intake mounting a large 780-cfm Holley four-barrel. According to *Motor Trend*, "[This] engine should put the Chevelle SS right up front in the supercar market."

1967 SS 396

A blacked-out cove treatment finally appeared for 1967's SS 396, as did restyled simulated hood vents and reshuffled Super Sport script on the rear quarters. SS 396 mechanicals were near-complete carryovers, save for less output (350 horsepower) for the optional L34 396.

New options included GM's superb three-speed Turbo Hydra-Matic (M40) automatic transmission and power-assisted front disc brakes (J52). The J52 brakes featured 11-inch rotors and Bendix four-piston calipers. Making this option even more attractive were a set of Rally wheels incorporating

The 325-horsepower 396 Turbo-Jet was again standard for the SS 396 in 1967. The optional L34 396 was now rated at 350 horsepower, down 10 horses from 1966.

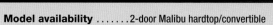

1967 SS 396

Model availability	2-door Malibu hardtop/convertible
Wheelbase	115 inches
Length	197 inches
Width	75 inches
Height	51.9 inches (hardtop), 52.8 inches (convertible)
Curb weight	3,800 pounds (hardtop)
Base price	$2,825 (hardtop), $3,033 (convertible)
Track	58 (front/rear, in inches)
Wheels	14 × 6
Tires	F70 × 14
Suspension	independent A-arms, coil springs & stabilizer bar in front; solid axle, upper/lower trailing arms, & coil springs in back
Steering	recirculating ball
Brakes	4-wheel drums
Transmission	3-speed manual, standard; 4-speed & Powerglide/Turbo-Hydra-Matic automatics, optional

Left: Convertible SS 396 production for 1967 was 3,321. Shown here are the new Rally wheels, which were included when the equally new optional front disc brakes were ordered. *GM*

Below: All Super Sport stuff, save for actual identification, was available for the Custom El Camino in 1966 and 1967. This 1967 El Camino not only wears the fake mag wheel covers made famous by 1965's Z16 Malibu, but it also is fitted with the 396 Turbo Jet V-8.

bright trim rings and center caps. Specially vented for the J52 application through slots in the rim center, the soon-to-be-popular Rally wheels measured the same as the stock 14 × 6 units. They were only available with the front disc brakes in 1967.

1968 SS 396

The A-body's 115-inch wheelbase was traded for a 112-inch stretch in 1968, at least for the two-door Malibu. Four-door Chevelles got a longer 116-inch chassis. On top of the frame in either case was a restyled body that looked considerably more like a Coke bottle. Though they lost 3 inches between their wheels, two-door Chevelles for 1968 remained about as long overall as their 1967 predecessors, meaning there now was some serious overhang up front, which helped make the lengthened 1968 hood appear even longer. At the same time, flush-mounted rear glass in place of 1967's recessed window further enhanced the shortened nature of the rear deck.

Contributing to the 1968 SS 396's new sleek look were hideaway windshield wipers, standard equipment for both the new luxury-minded Concours Chevelle and all Malibus. SS 396

1968 SS 396

Model availability	2-door Malibu hardtop/convertible & El Camino
Wheelbase	112 inches (Malibu); 116 inches (El Camino)
Length	197.1 inches (Malibu)
Width	75.7 inches (Malibu)
Height	52.7 inches (hardtop); 53.2 inches (convertible)
Weight	3,844 pounds (hardtop)
Base price	$2,875 (hardtop); $3,102 (convertible)
Track	59 (front/rear, in inches)
Wheels	14 × 6 stamped-steel
Tires	F70 × 14
Suspension	independent A-arms, coil springs & stabilizer bar in front; solid axle, upper/lower trailing arms, & coil springs in back
Steering	recirculating ball
Brakes	4-wheel drums
Transmission	3-speed manual, standard; 4-speed & Powerglide/Turbo Hydra-Matic automatics, optional

exterior treatment carried over in similar fashion with two exceptions: gone was the rear quarter script, and engine identification was now relegated to an almost unnoticeable tag incorporated within the side marker lamp bezels

Opposite: A full-fledged SS 396 El Camino finally appeared in 1968. Production of this high-powered hauler was 5,190. *GM*

Below: A new Coke-bottle Chevelle body appeared for 1968, as did a shorter wheelbase for the two-door Malibu: 112 inches, compared to the previously used 115-inch stretch. Notice the red D96 stripes on this 1968 SS 396.

1968 EL CAMINO SS 396

Model availability . . . . 2-door utility vehicle
Wheelbase . . . . 116 inches
Length . . . . 207.1 inches
Width . . . . 75.7 inches
Height . . . . 55.2 inches
Weight . . . . 3,930 pounds
Base price $2,949
Track . . . . 59 (front/rear, in inches)
Wheels . . . . 14 × 6 stamped-steel
Tires . . . . G70 × 14
Suspension . . . . independent A-arms, coil springs & stabilizer bar in front; solid axle, upper/lower
trailing arms, & coil springs in back
Steering . . . . recirculating ball
Brakes . . . . 4-wheel drums
Transmission . . . . 3-speed manual, standard; 4-speed and Powerglide/Turbo Hydra-Matic
automatics, optional

up front, new features for 1968 inspired by ever-tightening federal safety standards. A contrasting lower body treatment also was new this year for the SS 396.

Mechanicals were once again familiar, with 1967's three 396 V-8s offered at the same output levels.

1968 El Camino SS 396

Introduced in 1959, Chevrolet's half-car/half-truck rolled into temporary retirement in 1960 but was reborn on the new A-body platform in 1964. Initially available with nearly every option that helped make its Chevelle running mate such an overnight sensation, the downsized El Camino played as well as it worked. Like Chevelle, El Camino could be fitted with a host of hot small-blocks in 1964 and 1965 right up to the 350-horsepower L79. But the early A-body El Camino couldn't wear Super Sport garb. Even the 396 big-block was an option in 1966, as were bucket seats, a console, and the SS 396 Chevelle's mag-style wheel covers. Yet the complete SS image remained unavailable.

All that changed in 1968 when Chevrolet introduced an honest-to-goodness El Camino

SS 396, complete with those revered badges, an attractive blacked-out grille, and that bulging hood. "Fancier than a truck, more utilitarian than a passenger car, able to leap past sports car in a single bound, the El Camino [SS 396] will fill needs that the owner never knew he had." Or so claimed a *Car Life* report, which posted an impressive quarter-mile time of 14.80 seconds for the latest member of the Super Sport fraternity.

1969 SS 396

The leader of Detroit's muscle car pack since its 1964 intro, Pontiac's GTO was finally upstaged on the sales leader board in 1969, both by Plymouth's second-edition Road Runner and the new favorite, Chevrolet's fifth Super Sport Chevelle. Making news that year as well was the new way Chevy packaged its A-body SS. In 1968, the lineup included a Malibu sport coupe, convertible, and El Camino. Beginning the following year, an SS 396 buyer had to check off RPO Z25, which was offered for those same three body styles, plus two new ones in the low-priced 300 series. Both the 300 Deluxe sport coupe and 300 Deluxe sedan could be transformed into an SS 396 in 1969, the only year a Super Sport Chevelle appeared as anything other than a top-of-the-line Malibu or Custom El Camino.

Priced at $347.60, RPO Z25 was basically the same 396 package offered from 1966 to 1968, with a couple of nice additions. Standard power still came from the 325-horsepower 396 backed by a

1969 SS 396

Model availability	2-door Malibu hardtop/convertible; 2-door 300 Deluxe sport coupe/sedan & El Camino
Wheelbase	112 inches (Malibu/300 Deluxe); 116 inches, El Camino
Length	196.9 inches (Malibu/300 Deluxe)
Width	76 inches (Malibu/300 Deluxe)
Height	52.8 inches (hardtop)
Curb weight	3,335 pounds (hardtop)
Price	RPO Z25 cost $347.60
Track	59 (front/rear, in inches)
Wheels	14 × 7 five-spoke
Tires	F70 × 14 Wide Oval
Suspension	independent upper/lower A-arms, coil springs & stabilizer bar in front; solid axle, upper/lower trailing arms, & coil springs in back
Steering	recirculating ball
Brakes	front discs, rear drums
Transmission	3-speed manual, standard; 4-speed & Powerglide/Turbo Hydra-Matic automatic, optional

three-speed manual, and a beefed-up chassis also remained. But standard, too, in 1969 were power front disc brakes and a set of new five-spoke SS wheels. The brakes consisted of 11-inch rotors and single-piston calipers, while the wheels featured small SS center caps and bright trim rings. Set off by chrome wheel opening moldings, these 14 × 7 rims were the only wheels available for 1969's SS

396 and represented a marked departure from the dog-dish caps that had been standard from 1966 to 1968.

As for morphing the mundane 300 Deluxe into an SS 396, this job required a few more parts switches here and there. First, roof rail drip gutters, larger taillight bezels, and the upper body accent stripe were added, as were upper and lower rear

Above: In 1969, the Super Sport package became an option, RPO Z25, available for Malibu sports coupes and convertible, Custom El Caminos, and (for the first and only time) 300 Deluxe coupes and sedans. Disc brakes were included in the Z25 deal.

Opposite: Adding the Z25 option to a 300 Deluxe coupe or sedan in 1969 required deleting various trim pieces, including rocker moldings and 300 Deluxe fender badges. Roof rail drip gutters and larger taillight bezels were added, as were upper and lower rear cove moldings, these to delineate the Super Sport's blacked-out cove panel. Along with vent windows in the doors and those B-pillar posts, the 300 Deluxe sedan SS 396 also featured one other oddity—exposed windshield wipers. Vent wings disappeared on Malibu models in 1968, the same year that hidden wipers were also introduced for the top-shelf Chevelle.

The preferred Turbo Hydra-Matic automatic transmission carried on alone into 1969 after the Powerglide option was finally deleted. The TH400 option also was made available behind the L78 (as demonstrated here) for the first time that year.

Right: That four-speed stick is connected to the optional M21 close-ratio gearbox. Vinyl-coated rubber floor covering was just one of various means used by the 300-series Chevelle to keep costs down.

Opposite: Chevrolet introduced the L89 aluminum-head option for the Chevelle Super Sport's L78 396 only in 1969. These weight-saving heads did not change the L78's 375-horsepower rating.

cove moldings. The 300 Deluxe's rocker moldings were deleted, and the 300 Deluxe fender script was, of course, traded for the new SS 396 badge.

Inside, the dash and steering wheel both got SS identification, but the 300 sedan door panels didn't—because the 300's doors had vent windows and the Malibu hardtops didn't, meaning a different panel was required by the former. And because only Malibu models featured hideaway windshield wipers, the wiper arms on the 300 Deluxe SS 396 didn't retract beneath the cowl edge of the twin-bulge Super Sport hood. From there, however, everything else was basic Z25, right down to the sport wheels at the corners and bright exhaust extensions in back.

No breakdowns are available, but suffice it to say that the 300 Deluxe SS 396 was a rare bird in 1969. And its 300 sedan running mate was indeed a queer duck—it was the only SS 396 model ever offered with a B-pillar post. All others were hardtops or convertibles.

New on the options list in 1969 were weight-saving aluminum cylinder heads (for the L78 only) and low-restriction chambered exhausts. Basically a set of flow-through pipes with eight sets of eleven baffles running their 45-inch length (two smaller baffled pipes were included farther back), chambered exhausts (RPO NC8) were street legal,

1964–1966 Chevelle/Malibu Super Sport Engines

Year	RPO	CID	Horsepower	Torque	Induction	CR
1964	Std. (6-cyl.)	194	120 at 4,400 rpm	177 at 2,400 rpm	1-barrel carb	8.5:1
	L61 (6-cyl.)	230	155 at 4,400 rpm	215 at 2,000 rpm	1-barrel carb	8.5:1
	Std. (V-8)	283	195 at 4,800 rpm	285 at 2,400 rpm	2-barrel carb	9.25:1
	L77	283	220 at 4,800 rpm	295 at 3,200 rpm	4-barrel carb	9.25:1
	L30[1]	327	250 at 4,400 rpm	350 at 2,800 rpm	4-barrel carb	10.5:1
	L74[1]	327	300 at 5,000 rpm	360 at 3,200 rpm	4-barrel carb	10.5:1
	L76[2]	327	365 at 6,200 rpm	350 at 4,000 rpm	4-barrel carb	11.0:1

[1]Midyear additions

[2]Corvette L76 V-8 was briefly offered early in 1964, then cancelled

Year	RPO	CID	Horsepower	Torque	Induction	CR
1965	Std. (6-cyl.)	194	120 at 4,400 rpm	177 at 2,400 rpm	1-barrel carb	8.5:1
	L26 (6-cyl.)	230	140 at 4,400 rpm	220 at 1,600 rpm	1-barrel carb	8.5:1
	Std. (V-8)	283	195 at 4,800 rpm	285 at 2,400 rpm	2-barrel carb	9.25:1
	L77[3]	283	220 at 4,800 rpm	295 at 3,200 rpm	4-barrel carb	9.25:1
	L30	327	250 at 4,400 rpm	350 at 2,800 rpm	4-barrel carb	10.5:1
	L74	327	300 at 5,000 rpm	360 at 3,200 rpm	4-barrel carb	10.5:1
	L79	327	350 at 5,800 rpm	360 at 3,600 rpm	4-barrel carb	11.0:1
	L37[4]	396	375 at 5,600 rpm	420 at 3,600 rpm	4-barrel carb	11.0:1

[3]Some reports claim L77 returned to RPO list in February 1965 after being replaced by L30 at beginning of model year, but no L77 283s showed up in 1965 production records.

[4]Included w/Z16 Malibu SS 396 package

Year	RPO	CID	Horsepower	Torque	Induction	CR
1966	Std.	396[5]	325 at 4,800 rpm	410 at 3,200 rpm	4-barrel carb	10.25:1
	L34	396	360 at 5,200 rpm	420 at 3,600 rpm	4-barrel carb	10.25:1
	L78	396	375 at 5,600 rpm	415 at 3,600 rpm	4-barrel carb	11.0:1

Base 325-horsepower 396 had 2-bolt main bearing caps; L34 & L78 had 4-bolt mains.

[5]Listed as RPO L35 on Custom El Camino options list

although the local constabulary may have been more than willing to question that fact. Reportedly, chambered exhausts were included with the L34 396 before December 1968 and then were moved to the options list.

F41 sport suspension was introduced at extra cost in 1969 as well, which did the existing heavy-duty option one better. Offered for the Chevelle since 1964, the F40 package simply stiffened the springs and shocks. RPO F41 traded the 0.937-inch front sway bar for an unyielding 1.125-inch unit and also added a 0.875-inch rear stabilizer bar, along with special-duty bushings, reinforced lower control arms in back, and beefier springs and shocks.

Additional changes came in the transmission lineup, where the optional Powerglide was finally deleted, leaving the preferred Turbo Hydra-Matic to carry the load. And Turbo Hydra-Matics also were offered behind the brutal L78 for the first time, as were all manuals, including the special MC1 three-speed and M20 wide-ratio four-speed, gearboxes that previously had been spared the wrath of 375 hoppin'-mad horses. The M21 close-ratio four-speed remained L34 and L78 exclusives, and the

1969 COPO 9562

Model availability	2-door Malibu coupe/hardtop
Wheelbase	112 inches
Length	196.9 inches
Width	76 inches
Height	52.8 inches
Price	$4,100
Track	59 (front/rear, in inches)
Wheels	15 × 6 stamped-steel, 14 × 7 SS 5-spokes or 15 × 7 Rally rims
Tires	F70 × 14 or F70 × 15 Goodyear Wide Tread GT
Suspension	independent A-arms, heavy-duty coil springs & stabilizer bar in front; solid axle, upper/lower trailing arms, & heavy-duty coil springs in back
Steering	recirculating ball
Brakes	front discs, rear drums
Engine	425-horsepower 427-cubic-inch L72 V-8
Compression	11:1
Fuel delivery	800-cfm Holley 4-barrel carburetor
Transmission	4-speed manual or Turbo Hydra-Matic auto
Axle ratio	4.10:1 in heavy-duty 12-bolt axle with Positraction

M22 Rock Crusher, introduced in 1966, was again offered only along with RPO L78.

1969 COPO

The rule was plain enough: no engines larger than 400 cubes could be ordered for the Chevelle prior to 1970. What a shame, because the Corvette's 427-cubic-inch big-block could've slipped right in with only a few turns of a wrench. Performance products chief Vince Piggins knew how simple this swap was, and he also recognized a way to circumvent corporate policy to perform the switch right on a Chevrolet assembly line.

Piggins's trick involved COPO paperwork. Meant for special fleet orders by volume customers such as trucking firms and police departments, COPOs proved especially useful for Piggins because they didn't require upper-management approval. All that was needed was a go-ahead from the engineering office and almost any equipment combination became possible. Of course, if the process worked for trucks and cop cars, given a

little inside assistance, it could also be applied to performance automobiles.

Piggins first began considering the COPO loophole to produce 427-powered Camaros and Chevelles as early as July 1968. At the time, Pennsylvania Chevrolet dealer and former Chevy racer Don Yenko was marketing his own 427 Camaros and was looking both to expand into the Chevelle realm and make these packages easier to handle—easier by letting the factory take care of the engine swaps his mechanics had been performing since 1967. The result was the COPO 9561 Camaro, the factory-built 427 F-body used as a base for the Yenko Super Car conversion in 1969.

Yenko also began offering his S/C Chevelle that year, using COPOs to acquire specially equipped 427 A-bodies. Once he primed the COPO pump, 427 Chevelles became available to any Chevrolet customer in the know, although few recognized the opportunity. The COPO code in this case was 9562.

All COPO 9562 Chevelles relied on the 425-horsepower L72 Corvette 427 featuring 11:1

Above: As was the case on the outside, no clues existed beneath the hood as to a COPO Chevelle's true identity—notice the absence of any decals on the air cleaner lid of the 425-horsepower L72 427. Yenko Chevrolet re-rated the L72 at 450 horses for the COPO Chevelles it converted into Yenko S/C models.

Opposite: Although it has the blacked-out Super Sport grille, this mysterious '69 Chevelle is not an SS 396. It is a COPO car equipped with the Corvette's L72 427 V-8. The SS 396's hood with twin power bulges is also present. Estimates put production of 1969 COPO Chevelles at about 320 or so. Both hardtop and post-sedan models were built.

Above: Corvette-powered COPO Chevelles became Yenko Super Cars in 1969 at Don Yenko's dealership in Canonsburg, Pennsylvania. Yenko Chevrolet also offered 427-equipped Camaros and Novas that year, all adorned with similar striping.

Opposite: The name remained the same even after the Super Sport Chevelle's big-block was enlarged slightly to 402 cubic inches late in 1969. SS 396 coupes and convertibles continued rolling on into 1970.

compression, a 0.520-inch solid-lifter cam, big-valve heads (2.19-inch intakes, 1.72 exhausts), and a huge 800-cfm Holley four-barrel carb on an aluminum intake. Also included on the COPO 9562 High Performance Unit parts list was a heavy-duty radiator and the L72's oil pan, left-hand exhaust manifold, and clutch fork assembly and housing.

Completing the package was a special heavy-duty 12-bolt Positraction rear end with 4.10:1 gears and various beefed-up components. The Turbo Hydra-Matic 400 was available, while manual transmission choices included the M21 and M22 Rock Crusher four-speeds.

The COPO Chevelle's exterior left witnesses scratching their heads. The SS 396's twin-bulge hood, blacked-out grille and rear cove panel, D96 upper-body accent stripes, and chrome exhaust extensions were all included, but the cars weren't Super Sports. No SS exterior nomenclature appeared anywhere, nor was the 427's presence tipped off by an emblem or decal, not even under the hood. Although a few 427 Chevelles apparently came with SS steering wheels, basically all remaining features were pure Malibu. Contrary

to the quasi-SS look given these COPO cars, at least one 427 Chevelle came with Malibu lower-body trim.

Also contrary to 1969 SS 396 specifications, most COPO Chevelles rolled on 15 × 7 Rally wheels. Fourteen-inch Rallys were a Malibu option in 1969, but Super Sports came only with the exclusive 14 × 7 five-spoke SS rim, which some COPO cars did use. Optional 15-inch COPO tires, RPO ZP1, also were offered and would've included either standard 6-inch-wide rims with hubcaps or the wider Rally wheels. Reportedly never used on any other Chevrolet products, ZP1 tires were four-ply Goodyear Polyglas F70-15s with "Goodyear Wide Tread GT" in raised white letters.

According to Chevy big-block expert Fran Preve, Tonawanda engine plant records show 277

L-72 427s were produced for MQ-code manual-transmission COPO 9562 applications, while another 96 MP-code L-72s were intended for use with Turbo Hydra-Matics. But this combined total, 373, represents engines manufactured, not cars built. Speculating a bit, Preve estimated that perhaps as many as 323 COPO Chevelles were released, with ninety-nine of those known to have gone from the Baltimore assembly plant to Yenko Chevrolet in Canonsburg, Pennsylvania.

1970 SS 396

Listed again as RPO Z25, the SS 396 package for 1970 regained some of its earlier exclusivity as it once more was offered only for Custom El Caminos and Malibu hardtops and convertibles. No more post sedans. Along with revised exterior touches (for a nicely freshened Chevelle body), the Z25 deal included front disc brakes, F70 rubber on 14 × 7 SS wheels, bright wheelhouse trim, dual exhausts with chrome extensions, and appropriate interior

continued on page 105

1970 SS 396/454

Model availability	2-door Malibu hardtop/convertible & El Camino
Wheelbase	112 inches (Malibu); 116 inches (El Camino)
Length	197.2 inches (Malibu)
Width	76 inches (Malibu)
Height	52.8 inches (hardtop)
Weight	3,990 pounds (hardtop)
Price	RPO Z25 (SS 396) cost $445.55; RPO Z15 (SS 454) cost $503.4
Track	59 (front/rear, in inches)
Wheels	14 × 7 5-spoke
Tires	F70 × 14
Suspension	independent A-arms, coil springs & stabilizer bar in front; solid axle, upper/lower trailing arms, coil springs & stabilizer bar in back
Steering	recirculating ball
Brakes	front discs, rear drums
Transmission	4-speed manual or Turbo Hydra-Matic automatic

1967–1973 Chevelle/Malibu Super Sport Engines

Year	RPO	CID	Horsepower	Torque	Induction	CR
1967	Std.	396[6]	325 at 4,800 rpm	410 at 3,200 rpm	4-barrel carb	10.25:1
	L34	396	350 at 5,200 rpm	415 at 3,200 rpm	4-barrel carb	10.25:1
	L78	396	375 at 5,600 rpm	415 at 3,600 rpm	4-barrel carb	11.0:1

Base 325-horsepower 396 had 2-bolt main bearing caps; L34 & L78 had 4-bolt mains.

[6]Listed as RPO L35 on Custom El Camino options list

Year	RPO	CID	Horsepower	Torque	Induction	CR
1968	Std. (L35)	396	325 at 4,800 rpm	410 at 3,200 rpm	4-barrel carb	10.25:1
	L34	396	350 at 5,200 rpm	415 at 3,200 rpm	4-barrel carb	10.25:1
	L78	396	375 at 5,600 rpm	415 at 3,600 rpm	4-barrel carb	11.0:1

Base 325-horsepower 396 had 2-bolt main bearing caps; L34 & L78 had 4-bolt mains.

Year	RPO	CID	Horsepower	Torque	Induction	CR
1969	L35[7]	396[8]	325 at 4,800 rpm	410 at 3,200 rpm	4-barrel carb	10.25:1
	L34	396[8]	350 at 5,200 rpm	415 at 3,200 rpm	4-barrel carb	10.25:1
	L78	396[8]	375 at 5,600 rpm	415 at 3,600 rpm	4-barrel carb	11.0:1
	L72	427	425 at 5,000 rpm	460 at 4,000 rpm	4-barrel carb	11.0:1

Base 325-horsepower 396 had 2-bolt main bearing caps; L34 & L78 had 4-bolt mains.

[7]Included w/RPO Z25, the SS 396 package for Malibu, 300 Deluxe & Custom El Camino

[8]396-cubic-inch Mk IV V-8 was overbored to 402 cubic inches very late in the model run.

RPO L89 added aluminum heads to the L78 with no change in advertised output.

RPO L72 was Corvette V-8 used as part of the COPO 9562 high-performance unit.

Year	RPO	CID	Horsepower	Torque	Induction	CR
1970	L34[9]	402[10]	350 at 5,200 rpm	415 at 3,400 rpm	4-barrel carb	10.25:1
	L78	402[10]	375 at 5,600 rpm	415 at 3,600 rpm	4-barrel carb	11.0:1
	LS5[11]	454	360 at 5,400 rpm	500 at 3,200 rpm	4-barrel carb	10.25:1
	LS6	454	450 at 5,600 rpm	500 at 3,600 rpm	4-barrel carb	11.0:1

[9]Included w/RPO Z25, the SS 396 package for Malibu & Custom El Camino

[10]L34 & L78 V-8s were still called 396 Turbo Jets despite displacement increase.

[11]Included w/RPO Z15, the SS 454 package for Malibu & Custom El Camino

RPO L89 added aluminum heads to the L78 with no change in advertised output.

LS5 454 had 2-bolt main bearing caps; LS6 had 4-bolt mains.

Year	RPO	CID	Horsepower	Torque	Induction	CR
1971	L65[1]	350	245 at 4,800 rpm	350 at 2,800 rpm	2-barrel carb	8.5:1
	L48[1]	350	270 at 4,800 rpm	360 at 3,200 rpm	4-barrel carb	8.5:1
	LS3[2]	402	300 at 4,800 rpm	400 at 3,200 rpm	4-barrel carb	8.5:1
	LS5[3]	454	365 at 4,800 rpm	465 at 3,200 rpm	4-barrel carb	8.5:1

[1]Small-blocks used single exhaust; big-blocks used duals.

[2]Identified as Turbo Jet 400, also available for Heavy Chevy Chevelle

[3]Only the LS5 Chevelle carried full external identification (SS 454)—all other 1971 Super Sports, big- or small-block, were simply labeled SS.

All V-8s, small- or big-block, were offered as part of RPO Z15, the SS package for Malibu and Custom El Camino.

Year	RPO	CID	Horsepower	Torque	Induction	CR
1972	Std.[1]	307[3]	130 at 4,000 rpm	230 at 2,400 rpm	2-barrel carb	8.5:1
	L65[1]	350	165 at 4,000 rpm	280 at 2,400 rpm	2-barrel carb	8.5:1
	L48[1]	350	175 at 4,000 rpm	280 at 2,400 rpm	4-barrel carb	8.5:1
	LS3[2]	402[3]	240 at 4,400 rpm	345 at 3,200 rpm	4-barrel carb	8.5:1
	LS5[4]	454[3]	270 at 4,000 rpm	390 at 3,200 rpm	4-barrel carb	8.5:1

[1]Small-blocks used single exhaust; big-blocks used duals.

[2]Identified as Turbo Jet 400; also available for Heavy Chevy Chevelle

[3]Not available in California

[4]Only the LS5 Chevelle carried full external identification (SS 454)—all other 1972 Super Sports, big- or small-block, were simply labeled SS.

All V-8s, small- or big-block, were offered as part of RPO Z15, the SS package for Malibu and Custom El Camino.

All output figures beginning in 1972 were net-rated.

Year	RPO	CID	Horsepower	Torque	Induction	CR
1973	L65	350	145 at 4,000 rpm	255 at 2,400 rpm	2-barrel carb	8.5:1
	L48	350	175 at 4,000 rpm	260 at 2,800 rpm	4-barrel carb	8.5:1
	LS4	454	245 at 4,000 rpm	375 at 2,800 rpm	4-barrel carb	8.5:1

All V-8s, small- or big-block, were offered as part of RPO Z15, the SS package for Malibu Colonnade coupe, Malibu station wagons, and Custom El Camino.

Left: Super Sport El Caminos came with SS steering wheels like their 1970 Chevelle cousins. But they didn't get the SS 396/454 door panel emblems because they had vent windows—the required hand crank took the spot where the emblem belonged. Malibu coupes and convertibles for 1970 did not have vent windows, and thus had room for the extra interior identification.

Below: LS6 Chevelles actually outnumbered their tamer LS5 brothers in 1970. Production for the 360-horsepower LS5 SS 454 was 4,298. Chevrolet built 4,475 LS6 models that year. Estimates for LS6 convertibles range from 20 to 70. Also notice the absence of commonly seen hood stripes and cowl induction on this topless LS6.

Continued from page 101

identification. New standard features included an aggressive domed hood, exclusive Super Sport instrumentation borrowed from the Monte Carlo, and the coveted F41 sport suspension.

Z25 buyers in 1970 also could choose between an M20 four-speed or TH400 automatic—no three-speed, heavy-duty or otherwise, was available. Standard SS 396 power now came from the 350-horsepower L34 big-block as the L35 didn't return. The optional 375-horsepower L78 carried over one more time for its final appearance. Optional L89 aluminum heads returned as well but were cancelled early in the year.

Other intriguing options included RPOs D88 and ZL2. D88 was a sport stripe kit, which first appeared late in 1969. Featuring twin contrasting stripes (either black or white) running over the hood and rear deck, the D88 kit proved to be far more desirable than previous Super Sport stripe treatments.

The D88 stripes were added when the ZL2 option, the legendary cowl induction hood, was ordered. Featuring a vacuum-operated flap at the rear of yet another bulge stacked on top of the already bulging

SS hood, the ZL2 lid allowed cooler, denser outside air from the high-pressure area that normally develops at a windshield's base to force its way into the four-barrel below whenever the hammer went down. Underneath, a large rubber ring sealed a special open-element air cleaner to the cowl induction hood's dirty side. During normal operation, the carb drew air through a typical snorkel. But when the revs jumped and that flap opened, the ZL2 ductwork supplied as much air as the big-block could suck, helping an SS 396 blow the competition away.

1970 SS 454 CHEVELLE

By 1970, the SS 396 legacy had become so revered that Chevrolet's hype-masters didn't dare toy with it after the Turbo Jet big-block was bored out to 402 cubic inches late in 1969. "Ess-ess-four-oh-two?" No way. It was "Ess-Ess-three-ninety-six" or nothing at all. Unless, of course it was the new SS 454, the supreme evolution of the Chevelle Super Sport breed.

The Chevelle/El Camino SS 454 was born after GM finally dropped its 400-cubic-inch maximum

displacement limit for its intermediate models. Two widely different SS 454s were offered, by way of RPO Z15, for 1970, beginning with the relatively tame LS5 version with its 360 horsepower. The other featured the awesome LS6, a big-block bully that *Car Life* called "the best supercar engine ever released by General Motors." Many other critics considered the LS6 to be the best supercar engine, period.

Constructed with precision at GM's production plant in Tonawanda, New York, the LS6 454 was specially built from oil pan to air cleaner with truly super performance in mind. Unlike the LS5, which was based on a two-bolt main bearing block, the LS6's bottom end was held together with four-bolt main bearing caps. The crank was a tuftrided, forged 5140 alloy-steel piece cross-drilled to ensure ample oil supply to the connecting rod bearings. Rods were forged steel, magnafluxed, and equipped with $7/16$-inch bolts, compared to the LS5's $3/8$-inch units. At the rods' business ends were TRW forged-aluminum pistons, which mashed the mixture at a ratio of 11.25:1. LS5 compression was 10.25:1. An aggressive

Left: The dual-snorkel air cleaner on this LS6 454 is the rarest of the three different units used in 1970. This type of an open-element air cleaner (with chrome lid) was used whenever the cowl induction option wasn't chosen.

Opposite top: Standard for 1970's SS 396, Malibu or El Camino, was a 350-horsepower big-block. Optional muscle was supplied by the 375-horsepower L78 396. An El Camino application appears here.

Opposite bottom: The Z25 SS 396 package was priced at $455.15 for 1970's Custom El Camino.

Above: The SS 454 package was listed under RPO Z15 in 1970. Available for Malibu coupes and convertibles and the Custom El Camino, the Z15 option was priced at $503. Along with typical badges, the SS 454 package also added wheel opening moldings, a black-accented grille, and exclusive sport wheels in 1970. A black resilient rear panel also was included in the El Camino's case.

Right: Tame in comparison to its 450-horsepower big brother, the LS5 nonetheless was no wimp. Rated at 360 horsepower, the milder 454 Mk IV, with its hydraulic lifters, was much easier to live with in everyday use.

cam (0.520-inch lift, 316-degree duration) activated solid lifters.

On top were free-breathing closed-chamber cylinder heads with large rectangular ports and big valves: 2.19-inch intakes and 1.88-inch exhausts. A 780-cfm Holley four-barrel fed this beast, which was conservatively rated at 450 horsepower, the highest advertised output figure ever assigned to a muscle car engine. Some claim actual output was more than 500 horses. Whatever the truth, results on the street were earth-shaking.

"Driving a 450-horsepower Chevelle is like being the guy who's in charge of triggering atom bomb tests," claimed a *Super Stock* report. "You have the power, you know you have the power, and you know if you use the power, bad things may happen. Things like arrest, prosecution, loss of license, broken pieces, shredded tires, etc." Finishing the quarter mile in a tad more than

thirteen seconds was no problem for the LS6. "That's LS as in Land Speed Record," concluded *Motor Trend*'s A. B. Shuman.

Even though the 450-horsepower 454 alone cost $1,000 extra, the slightly cranky LS6-powered Chevelle actually outsold its more affordable LS5 brother, 4,475 to 4,298.

1970 Monte Carlo SS454

General manager Pete Estes (who had replaced Bunkie Knudsen at Chevrolet in July 1965) put his head together with chief designer David Holls to create the Monte Carlo, which was introduced in September 1969 by Estes's successor, John DeLorean. More or less a stretched Chevelle, the relatively luxurious Monte Carlo was inspired by the Grand Prix, itself a lengthened version of Pontiac's A-body (redefined as a G-car) first seen in 1969.

Production of Chevrolet's first Monte Carlo was 145,975, most of them powered by 350 small-blocks in 1970.

Adding RPO Z20 meant trading that 350 for the LS5 454 big-block, resulting in what *Car Life* called a "gentleman's bomb," the SS454 Monte Carlo. Along with the LS5, the $420 Z20 package included a heavy-duty suspension (stiffer springs and shocks, front and rear sway bars, and air-regulated Automatic Level Control) and G70 tires on 15 × 7 wheels. Outward identification consisted only of twin chrome exhaust tips and black-accented rocker trim incorporating appropriate lettering.

Front disc brakes were standard for all Monte Carlos, and the Turbo Hydra-Matic automatic

Car Life called 1970's new SS454 Monte Carlo a "gentleman's bomb." A vinyl roof was optional.

Beneath the SS454 Monte Carlo's long, long hood was the 360-horsepower LS5 big-block. A heavy-duty suspension with front and rear sway bars also was standard.

1970 MONTE CARLO SS454

Model availability	2-door coupe
Wheelbase	116 inches
Length	205.8 inches
Width	75.6 inches
Height	52.9 inches
Curb weight	4,140 pounds
Base price	RPO Z20 cost $420.25
Track	59 (front/rear, in inches)
Wheels	15 × 7
Tires	G70 × 15
Suspension	independent A-arms, coil springs & stabilizer bar in front; solid axle, upper/lower trailing arms, coil springs & stabilizer bar in back
Steering	recirculating ball
Brakes	front discs, rear drums
Engine	360-horsepower 454-cubic-inch LS5 Turbo Jet V-8
Transmission	Turbo Hydra-Matic automatic, standard

was a mandatory addition (costing another $222) for the SS454. Some four-speed manuals may have been installed by special order. Popular options included a vinyl roof, air conditioning, power windows, floorshift with console, special instrumentation, simulated woodgrain dash, and Strato bucket seats.

1971

Only one SS equipment group, RPO Z15, was listed for 1971's Chevelle, which featured new single headlamps up front and a revised rear bumper that now incorporated two round taillights at each end. Priced at $357, this package included power front disc brakes, F41 sports suspension with rear stabilizer bar, black-accented grille, domed hood, special instrument panel,

Above: Strato bucket seats were optional inside the SS454 Monte Carlo. GM's Turbo Hydra-Matic automatic transmission was a mandatory option. Some sources claim a few four-speed manuals also might have been installed.

Left: The SS 454 remained the king of the midsized Super Sport lineup in 1971 and again was offered in hardtop or convertible forms.

and bright wheel opening trim. New standard features included 15 × 7 five-spoke Camaro sport wheels wearing F60 rubber, a remote-control left-hand mirror, and competition-style hood pins. The latter items were previously seen in 1970 when the cowl induction hood was installed. Both the ZL2 and D88 options carried over from the previous year.

The biggest news for 1971 involved the return of small-block power, the first in Chevelle Super Sport ranks in six years. Engine choices now numbered four: two 350-cubic-inch small-blocks and two Mk IV big-blocks. Rated at 245 horsepower, the L65 350 featured 8.5:1 compression as well as two items Chevelle SS buyers also hadn't seen

Below: New single headlamps set 1971's Chevelle apart from its predecessors. Only one Super Sport equipment group, RPO Z15, was offered this year, and an available small-block V-8 returned. Only the SS 454 received its own individual exterior identification in 1971. This SS convertible, powered by the LS3 big-block, wears the same SS badges seen on small-block models that year.

1971 SS

Model availability	2-door Malibu hardtop/convertible & El Camino
Wheelbase	112 inches (Malibu); 116 inches (El Camino)
Length	197.5 inches (Malibu)
Width	75.4 inches (Malibu)
Height	52.7 inches (hardtop)
Curb weight	3,670 pounds (small-block hardtop)
Base price	RPO Z15 cost $357.05
Track	60/59.9 (front/rear, in inches)
Wheels	15 × 7 5-spoke (Camaro sport-type)
Tires	F60 × 15
Suspension	independent A-arms, coil springs & stabilizer bar in front; solid axle, upper/lower trailing arms, coil springs & stabilizer bar in back
Steering	recirculating ball
Brakes	front discs, rear drums
Transmission	3-speed manual, standard; 4-speed & Powerglide/Turbo Hydra-Matic automatics, optional

Above: The 402-cubic-inch LS3 big-block was rated at 300 horsepower in 1971. Notice the absence of an air cleaner decal, a sure sign of changing times.

Left: The Heavy Chevy Chevelle was introduced midyear in 1971. It offered some of the Super Sport's flair at a lower cost. All V-8s except the LS5 454 were available beneath the Heavy Chevy's domed hood.

since 1965: a two-barrel carburetor and single exhaust. The L48 350 also used 8.5:1 compression and a single tailpipe but traded that two-barrel for a four-barrel. L48 output was 270 horsepower. The big-blocks were the 300-horsepower Turbo Jet 400 (which actually displaced 402 cubic inches) and the surviving LS5 454, now rated at 365 horsepower. Although magazines did road test a 1971 LS6-powered Chevelle, it failed to make it into regular production.

Transmission choices varied by powerplant. The L65 was backed by either the TH 350 automatic or M20 wide-ratio four-speed. The M11 three-speed manual was the base box behind the L48, while the MC1 heavy-duty three-speed was standard for the LS3 big-block. The M40 TH400 automatic and M20 four-speed were LS3 options. LS5 buyers got to choose between the TH400 and M22 Rock Crusher four-speed.

Gone was the revered SS 396 badge. Chevelle Super Sport fenders in 1971 simply wore SS emblems in small- or big-block applications, unless the LS5 was installed. SS 454 identification remained for Chevrolet's biggest big-block.

The SS454 Monte Carlo made an encore appearance in 1971. New Super Sport identification appeared in a black band at the tail.

1971 MONTE CARLO SS454

Model availability	2-door coupe
Wheelbase	116 inches
Length	205.8 inches
Width	75.6 inches
Height	52.9 inches
Weight	4,195 pounds
Base price	RPO Z20 cost $484.50
Track	59 (front/rear, in inches)
Wheels	15 × 7 Rally
Tires	G70 × 15
Suspension	independent A-arms, coil springs & stabilizer bar in front; solid axle, upper/lower trailing arms, coil springs & stabilizer bar in back
Steering	recirculating ball
Brakes	front discs, rear drums
Transmission	Turbo Hydra-Matic automatic, standard

Above: The SS454 Monte Carlo received appropriate identification at its tail in 1971.

Below: The mighty LS6 didn't survive into 1971, at least not in Chevelles (it became a Corvette-only option that year), but the LS5 did. Advertised LS5 output for 1971 was 365 horsepower.

Below: El Camino again represented different types of transportation for different types of drivers in 1971. Even in base form, it was a classy hauler. But after adding the Z15 Super Sport equipment and a 454 V-8, a buyer could've given "hauling" all new meaning. *GM*

Bottom: Chevrolet's excellent F41 suspension (with rear stabilizer bar) and front disc brakes remained a part of the Z15 package in 1972. This 1972 SS hardtop is fitted with the 402-cubic-inch LS3 V-8, rated at 240 horsepower.

1971 Monte Carlo SS454

The Monte Carlo SS454 returned for 1971, this time with 365 standard horses. New this year was a black band across the back featuring a small SS badge on the right. Special suspension components carried over from 1970, as did the G70 rubber. But 15 × 7 Rally wheels were not specified as standard equipment—the wide rims listed for the first Monte Carlo 454 may or may not have been Rally units. While an optional 454 big-block remained a Monte Carlo option after 1971, the SS454 package did not return.

1972

Save for restyled front marker lights and a new grille that now encompassed the headlights, 1972's Chevelle was a near-perfect copy of its 1971 predecessor. And other than a color-keyed remote-control left-hand sport mirror in place of the 1971's plated unit, the Z15 package rolled over almost identically too. The most notable change came where it hurt, as all Chevelle V-8s, including the truly meek Turbo Fire 307 small-block, became available for the 1972 SS.

The sporty four-spoke steering wheel shown here was a Chevelle SS option in 1972. Eagle eyes might also notice the optional 7,000-rpm tachometer.

1972 SS

Model availability	2-door Malibu hardtop/convertible & El Camino
Wheelbase	112 inches (Malibu); 116 inches (El Camino)
Length	197.5 inches (Malibu)
Width	75.4 inches (Malibu)
Height	52.7 inches (hardtop)
Curb weight	3,650 pounds (small-block hardtop)
Base price	RPO Z15 cost $357.05
Track	60/59.9 (front/rear, in inches)
Wheels	15 × 7 5-spoke (Camaro sport-type)
Tires	F60 × 15
Suspension	independent A-arms, coil springs & stabilizer bar in front; solid axle, upper/lower trailing arms, coil springs & stabilizer bar in back
Steering	recirculating ball
Brakes	front discs, rear drums
Transmission	3-speed manual, standard; 4-speed & Powerglide/Turbo Hydra-Matic automatics, optional

Above: Revised trim that completely encompassed the Super Sport's blacked-out grille and headlights appeared in 1972. Again, non-discriminatory SS badges were used for both 350- and 402-equipped models. This 1972 SS convertible features the 350 small-block.

Right: Standard power for 1972's Chevelle SS was a 130-horsepower 307-cubic-inch small-block. The optional L65 350 was net-rated at 165 horsepower, and its L48 running mate at 175.

Above: This convertible is one of 1,625 SS 454 Chevelles built for 1972 with the M22 Rock Crusher four-speed manual transmission.

Left: Chevrolet's optional LS5 454 was rated at 270 horsepower in 1972. Compression was a comfortable 8.5:1.

As in 1971, all 1972 SS engines featured 8.5:1 compression. Net outputs were 130 horsepower for the 307-cubic-inch small-block, 165 for the L65, 175 for the L48, 240 for the LS3 big-block, and 270 for the LS5 454. An available Powerglide returned for the 307, which, like the L65, was backed in standard form by a three-speed manual. Remaining transmission choices echoed those from 1971. Chevelle SS buyers in California could only order the two 350-cubic-inch small-block V-8s in 1972.

1973

A totally restyled Chevelle body debuted for 1973 and no longer featured a two-door hardtop variation. In its place was GM's Colonnade coupe, a sweeping, pillared roofline shared that year with Buick, Oldsmobile, and Pontiac. RPO Z15 carried over into this new age for one last fling (in Chevelle ranks; it rolled on for the El Camino into the 1980s) and this time was available for the Malibu Colonnade coupe and two Malibu station wagons: a six-passenger two-seater and its eight-passenger, three-seat companion. Nineteen-seventy-three was the only year an SS wagon was offered.

The Z15 package for 1973 included G70 tires on 14 × 7 Rally rims, dual sport mirrors, and a special instrument cluster with black bezels. SS identification appeared inside the door panels and steering wheel, while exterior dress-up included a blacked-out grille, color-keyed striping along the lower body sides and wheel openings, bright drip moldings, bright trim for the triangular rear-quarter windows, and SS badges for the grille, fenders, and tail. SS wagons also received a rear stabilizer bar.

The available engine list began with the L65 350 small-block, net-rated at 145 horsepower. Next was the L48 350, at 175 horses. Top dog was the LS4 454 big-block, which pumped out 245 ponies.

Above: Chevrolet last offered its SS 454 Chevelle/El Camino duo in 1972. All A-bodies built that year initially featured blacked-out headlight bezels (not visible here). But in December 1971, Malibu, Concours wagons, and Custom El Caminos switched to chromed bezels. *GM*

Opposite top: The Chevelle SS made a final appearance in 1973, this time based on Chevrolet's totally restyled Colonnade coupe. *GM*

Opposite bottom: El Camino continued accompanying its Chevelle cousin into the A-body's third-generation run in 1973. Along with being noticeably longer than its 1972 predecessor, Chevy's restyled 1973 El Camino also weighed considerably more—3,725 pounds, compared to about 3,450. *GM*

1973 SS

SS

Model availability	2-door Malibu Colonnade coupe/station wagon & El Camino
Wheelbase	113 inches
Base price	RPO Z15 cost $242.75
Wheels	14 × 7 Rally
Tires	G70 × 14
Suspension	independent A-arms, coil springs & stabilizer bar in front; solid axle, upper/lower trailing arms, coil springs & stabilizer bar (for the SS station wagon) in back
Steering	recirculating ball
Brakes	front discs, rear drums
Transmission	3-speed manual, standard; 4-speed & Turbo Hydra-Matic automatic, optional

1964–1973 Chevelle/Malibu Super Sport Production Figures

1964	6-cyl. Hardtops	6-cyl. Convertibles	Line Total
	8,224	1,551	9,775
	V-8 Hardtops	V-8 Convertibles	
	57,445	9,640	67,085
	Grand Total		**76,860**
1965	6-cyl. Hardtops	6-cyl. Convertibles	
	7,452	1,133	8,585
	V-8 Hardtops	V-8 Convertibles	
	64,532	7,995	72,527
	Grand Total		**81,112**

Note: L79 production, in all 1965 Chevelles/El Caminos: 4,716

1965 Z16 Malibu SS 396	Hardtop	Convertible	
	200	1	**201***

*According to National Chevelle Owners Association founder Mark Meekins, one 1965 Chevelle, a 300-series sedan, also was built with a COPO-installed 425-horsepower 396 Turbo Jet.

1966	SS 396 Hardtops	SS 396 Convertibles	
	66,843	5,429	**72,272**

RPO Breakdowns

L35 325-horsepower 396 Turbo Jet, for Custom El Camino	1,865
L34 360-horsepower 396 Turbo Jet, for SS 396 Chevelle/Custom El Camino	24,811
L78 375-horsepower 396 Turbo Jet, for SS 396 Chevelle/Custom El Camino	3,099
M22 "Rock Crusher" 4-speed transmission	12
L79 350-horsepower 327 Turbo Fire, for non-SS Chevelles/El Caminos	7,591

1967	59,685	3,321	**63,006**

RPO Breakdowns

L35 325-horsepower 396 Turbo Jet, for Custom El Camino	2,565
L34 350-horsepower 396 Turbo Jet, for SS 396 Chevelle/Custom El Camino	17,176
L78 375-horsepower 396 Turbo Jet, for SS 396 Chevelle/Custom El Camino	612

1968	SS 396 Hardtops	SS 396 Convertibles	SS 396 El Camino	
	55,309	2,286	5,190	**62,785**

RPO Breakdowns

L34 350-horsepower 396 Turbo Jet	12,481
L78 375-horsepower 396 Turbo Jet	4,751
M22 "Rock Crusher" 4-speed transmission	1,049
L79 350-horsepower 327 Turbo Fire, for non-SS Chevelles/El Caminos	9,440

1969	RPO Z25, for Malibu[1], 300 Deluxe[2], and El Camino	**86,307**

RPO Breakdowns

L34 350-horsepower 396 Turbo Jet	17,358
L78 375-horsepower 396 Turbo Jet	9,486
L89 aluminum heads for L78 396	400
M22 "Rock Crusher" 4-speed transmission	1,276

[1]Sport coupe and convertible
[2]Sport coupe and sedan

1970	RPO Z25, SS 396 package[3]	**53,599**
	RPO Z15, SS 454 package[3]	8,773
	Grand Total	**62,372**

[3]For Malibu coupes/convertibles and El Caminos

RPO Breakdowns

L34 350-horsepower 396 Turbo Jet (actually displaced 402 cubic inches)	51,437
L78 375-horsepower 396 Turbo Jet (actually displaced 402 cubic inches)	2,144
L89 aluminum heads for L78 396	18
LS5 360-horsepower 454 Turbo Jet	4,298
LS6 450-horsepower 454 Turbo Jet	4,475
M22 "Rock Crusher" 4-speed transmission	5,410

1971	RPO Z15, SS package with small- or big-block V-8[4]	**19,293**
1972	RPO Z15, SS package with small- or big-block V-8[4]	**24,946**

[4]For Malibu coupes/convertibles and El Caminos

1973	RPO Z15, SS package with small- or big-block V-8[5]	**28,647**

Above: Chevrolet offered a Super Sport station wagon for one year only, 1973. Turbine wheels were standard for this gonzo grocery-getter. *GM*

Left: The Laguna S-3 coupe replaced the Chevelle SS for 1974. *GM*

HORSEPLAY

Chevrolet Camaro SS: 1967–1972

Fifty years ago Ford's original Mustang owned the road. Nothing in the affordable compact arena could compare, not even Plymouth's Valiant-based Barracuda, the little fun machine that actually burst out of the gates first in April 1964. The innovative vehicle that helped inspire the Mustang, Chevrolet's sporty Corvair Monza, was never a threat, nor was the diminutive Chevy II, its stylish Super Sport alter-ego notwithstanding. Any hopes of disrupting this one-horse race hinged on GM's development of its own new breed. It was time to saddle up.

▶ Camaros were built in two plants from 1967 to 1971: in Norwood, Ohio, and Van Nuys, California. Only Norwood rolled out Camaros from 1972 to 1975. F-body production restarted at Van Nuys in February 1976, and both plants again shared the load until the Norwood plant closed in 1987. Van Nuys carried on alone up through 1992.

▶ The Camaro legacy now consists of six generations: 1967 to 1969, 1970 to 1981, 1981 to 1992, 1993 to 2002, 2010 to 2015, and 2016 to present.

▶ Journalists became acquainted with Chevrolet's sixth production model on September 12, 1966, as Camaro officially joined Corvair, Chevy II, Chevelle, Corvette, and the full-sized group.

▶ Chevrolet's biggest small-block V-8 to date, at 350 cubic inches, debuted for 1967, but only beneath Camaro hoods, and only as part of the Super Sport package. All other Chevys (except, of course, for the Corvair) started offering the optional 350 V-8 in 1968.

▶ The Super Sport Camaro retired after 1972 and was replaced by the Type LT.

Plans for a suitable competitor began percolating in the summer of 1964. Recognizing a new sensation when he saw it, Henry Haga in Chevrolet Number Two Studio already had finished several sketches when general manager Bunkie Knudsen got the go-ahead in August to add yet another new model to an already crowded lineup.

A few years earlier, Knudsen had actually *declined* Herb Rybicki's idea for a relatively upscale personal coupe based on the Chevy II, claiming that he liked the proposal loads, but the company simply didn't need another new model, not with Chevrolet's fifth (Chevelle) then being readied for its 1964 debut. As Rybicki later recalled, his proposal included much of the Mustang's makeup at a time when no one at GM even knew Ford's world-shaker was in the works. The same was true for the sensational Super Nova, another sporty proposal based on the Chevy II platform. Transformed from clay into running concept car by Haga's team late in 1963, the Super Nova was turning heads at the New York Auto Show a few weeks before the Mustang made its historic Big Apple debut at the 1964 World's Fair. This time Knudsen favored rushing to market, as did Mitchell and his predecessor, retired GM Styling mogul Harley Earl. Still, GM president Jack Gordon declined. In August 1964, Knudsen was instructed to have Chevrolet's direct response, called the F-car, up and running by the fall of 1966, a tight deadline for sure. Haga's studio wasted little time sculpting a prototype code-named XP-836.

Most of what became the final model appeared in December in the form of a full-sized clay. The hood was long, the rear deck short, and overall impressions were truly sporty. What set the F-car apart was its softly contoured shape, which instantly made Ford's original pony car look stiff and boxy in comparison. As for basic dimensions, the Mustang's new challenger was longer, lower, and wider, and featured a little more passenger room inside.

The sporty coupe would feature unibody construction beneath its beautiful exterior (once it was morphed into metal), similar to Mustang but with additional notable differences. Whereas the existing Ford was fully unitized with stamped-steel sections welded onto the body up front to carry the engine and suspension components, Chevrolet's newcomer featured a strong ladder-type front subframe that bolted up to the body. To help hit the short deadline, F-car project engineers simply borrowed this platform from the next-generation Chevy II being prepared for its 1968 introduction. Drivetrains also transferred over with no fuss/muss, as did the Chevy II's mono plate springs in back.

As for its name, company insiders at first called Chevy's new pony car Panther. But this tag didn't stick. Merchandising manager Bob Lund and GM Car and Truck Group vice president Ed Rollert put their heads together and came up with Camaro, a word that, in Lund's opinion, had "kind of a ring" to it. In French it meant friend, comrade, or pal.

Above: Chevrolet's markedly restyled Camaro for 1969 suited the Super Sport image to a T.

Previous pages: Left: Some GM execs wanted to put the Super Nova show car, widely publicized in 1964, into production as a response to Ford's Mustang.
Right: The 1967 Camaro SS coupe's silhouette is as handsome now—very much replicated in the 2016 50th Anniversary model—as it was when it debuted in 1967. *GM*

Opposite: Like Ford's original Mustang in 1964, Chevy's first Camaro also was invited to pace the Indy 500. And although not officially marketed as pace car replicas, about 160 look-alike models eventually found their ways into private owners' hands in 1967 after serving complimentary duties prior to the race. Like the actual SS/RS pacer, these convertibles were all done in blue-striped white paint and included either 350 Turbo Fire small-blocks or 396 Turbo Jet big-blocks. *GM*

Chevrolet general manager Pete Estes (who had taken over from Bunkie Knudsen in July 1965) officially announced the Camaro during a press conference in Detroit on June 29, 1966. He called it a "four-passenger package of excitement." He also explained how the French translation fit because "the real mission of our new automobile [is] to be a close companion to its owner, tailored to reflect his or her individual tastes." Like Mustang, Camaro was meant to represent different cars to different drivers, with a budget-conscious six-cylinder starting things off in the basic package. But a flair for fun was still the prime attraction, a fact Estes wasn't about to overlook. "The Camaro is aimed at the fast-growing personal sports-type market that was pioneered by Chevrolet's Corvette in 1953 and further defined by the Corvair Monza in the 1960s," Estes said.

Indeed, Camaro needed little time after its official press introduction on September 12, 1966, to impress witnesses with its wide-ranging sporting potential, which in some minds created quite a dilemma for Chevy

Opposite top: Thirty years of Camaro history was marked in 1997 by an appearance at Indianapolis as the pace car (seen in foreground) for NASCAR's Brickyard 400. Four other Camaros had previously paced the Indianapolis 500: (from left to right) in 1967, 1969, 1982, and 1993.

Opposite bottom: In 2002, Chevrolet's last fourth-generation Camaro was the thirty-fifth model of the breed, inspiring a special anniversary package for SS coupes and convertibles. Bright Rally Red paint was the only shade available for these commemorative models.

Above: The Super Sport Camaro made a triumphant return (along with all-new fifth-generation model) for 2010 and rolled into its sixth generation in 2016. The Corvette's 455-horsepower LT-1 V-8 powered the 2016 SS (shown here).

Left: Contrary to the Mustang's fully welded unitized body/frame platform, the Camaro's foundation featured an independent front subframe that bolted up to its body structure. Single-leaf springs were standard in back in 1967.

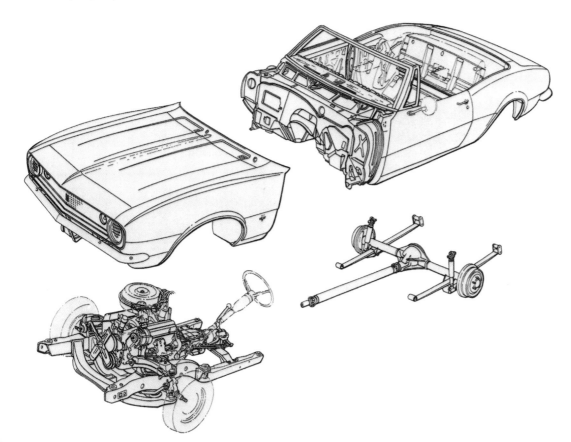

customers. "The problem is not whether to buy the Camaro," claimed a March 1967 *Car Life* report, "but what kind of Camaro, for [this model] probably wears more faces than any other single car now made."

The 327-cubic-inch V-8 was available from the beginning, as was the bigger, better 350 small-block, created by stroking the 327. The 350 was not only exclusive to Camaro in 1967, but it also was restricted to the Super Sport rendition, which everyone knew just had to make an appearance in keeping with yet another established tradition. Enhancing the Camaro SS attraction further was the Rally Sport package, a cosmetic option that included (among other doodads) trendy hideaway headlights. Additional choices included the SS 396 model, a big-block bully that appeared in November 1966 and acted more like a Clydesdale than a pony. A few weeks later the legendary Z28 also became part of the mix, stirring buyers' blood even more.

By New Year's Day 1967, Mustang drivers were the ones eating dust.

1967

Chevy's first Camaro was offered in coupe and convertible and was segregated into two lines— one with the base 230-cubic-inch Turbo-Thrift six-cylinder, the other with a standard 327-cube Turbo Fire V-8. Output for the latter was 210 horsepower. A 250-cubic-inch six and 275-horsepower 327 small-block were optional.

As mentioned, 1967's Camaro Super Sport came standard with the new 295-horsepower 350 V-8 topped by a four-barrel carburetor and dressed up with chrome pieces. One couldn't be had without the other, thus the whole package was listed under RPO L48, identified as the "Camaro SS w/ 295-horsepower Turbo-Fire 350-cubic-inch engine." The model was called the SS 350, though

that nomenclature only appeared on the grille and on the fuel filler cap. Simple SS identification showed up on the fenders. Additional dress-up touches included a color-keyed (black or white) accent stripe around the nose, and the rest of the SS deal consisted of a special hood with simulated vents, red-stripe Wide Oval tires on wider 14 × 6 JK wheels, and the F41 heavy-duty suspension.

Left: Ordering a Camaro SS in 1967 was achieved by checking off the RPO code for one of three available V-8s, beginning with the L48 350 Turbo Fire small-block.

Opposite top: Adding the Rally Sport package to a 1967 Super Sport Camaro meant hiding the headlights behind a fully blacked-out grille. Notice the pre-production body side stripe. *GM*

Opposite bottom: The Waikiki show car Camaro featured a surfboard rack, rattan seat inserts, and teakwood side panels. *GM*

Below: Chevy's new 350 V-8 was only offered for the Super Sport Camaro in 1967. The base price for the SS 350 package was $210.65.

Above: The 350 small-block was created by boring and stroking the 327 V-8, and it debuted between Camaro fenders in 1967. It appeared in other Chevrolet models the following year. Chrome dress-up was part of the Super Sport package. *David Kimble cutaway, courtesy GM*

Opposite top: The big-block SS 396 joined the Camaro lineup in November 1966 and instantly blew Ford's 390 Mustang away.

Opposite bottom left: A walnut-grained sport steering wheel was a $31.60 option in 1967.

Opposite bottom right: The U17 instrumentation option, available only in 1967 for console-equipped V-8 Camaros, added this gauge cluster, along with a tachometer. The price for the U17 option was $79.

A yeoman three-speed stick (on the column) was standard behind the L48 small-block. Drivetrain options included the beefed-up, floorshift M13 three-speed, the wide-ratio M20 four-speed, the close-ratio M21 four-speed, and the Powerglide automatic. Buyers also could add Chevy's new front disc brakes, which again included attractive Rally wheels. And let's not forget the aforementioned Rally Sport group, a popular package offered for all Camaro models in 1967.

Priced at $105.35, the snazzy RS option (RPO Z22) dressed up both ends of a coupe or convertible, with a distinctive rear taillamp treatment joining those electronically controlled disappearing headlights. RS taillights were solid red with flat-black trim compared to standard units that used bright trim and incorporated white backup lenses. On Rally Sport models, backup lights were moved down into the rear valance panel. The same was true for the turn signals up front, which also dropped down into the valance from their regular position in the grille.

Camaro Rally Sports were further adorned with lower bodyside moldings atop black-finished sills (deleted on certain dark-colored cars), bright wheel opening trim and roof drip moldings, and color-keyed upper bodyside stripes. Appropriate

badges were included too, though these were superseded whenever RPO Z22 was applied to a Super Sport Camaro—SS took precedence over RS.

The Z22 option was available for either Super Sport, small-, or big-block. Like the SS 350, the meaner, nastier SS 396 Camaro was identified in the options list by its engine code, beginning with RPO L35, the tag for the 325-horsepower hydraulic-lifter 396 V-8. A second Mk IV big-block—the bodacious 375-horsepower L78—was also offered, making Chevy's new pony car the undisputable leader of the pack. Ford's equally new big-block Mustang GT, with its comparably tame 390-cubic-inch FE-series V-8, simply was no match for an L78 Camaro in 1967.

Opposite: A poor man's Corvette? Not a bad description for a Camaro SS convertible, small-block or big, in 1968.

Below: The L35 396 big-block added $263.30 to a Camaro SS bottom line in 1967. L35 production that year was 4,003.

1967 CAMARO SS

Model availability	2-door sport coupe, 2-door convertible
Wheelbase	108 inches
Length	184.7 inches
Width	72.5 inches
Height	51.4 inches
Curb weight	3,269 pounds (SS 350 coupe)
Price	RPO L48 cost $210.65, RPO L35 cost $263.30, RPO L78 cost $500.30 (base V-8 coupe: $2,572; base V-8 convertible: $2,809)
Track	59/58.9 (front/rear, in inches)
Wheels	14 × 6 stamped-steel
Tires	D70 red-stripe Firestone
Suspension	independent unequal A-arms, coil springs & stabilizer bar in front; single-leaf springs, solid axle w/right-side traction bar in back
Steering	recirculating ball
Brakes	hydraulic drums, front & rear
Engine	290-horsepower 350-cubic-inch L48 V-8, 325-horsepower 396-cubic-inch L35 V-8, 375-horsepower 396-cubic-inch L78 V-8
Bore & stroke	4.00 × 3.48 inches, 350 V-8; 4.094 × 3.76 inches, 396 V-8
Compression	10.25:1 (L48 & L35 V-8s), 11:1 (L78 V-8)
Fuel delivery	single 4-barrel carburetor
Transmission	3-speed manual std. w/L48; special 3-speed std., w/L35 & L78

1968

Technical updates in 1968 included staggering the rear shock absorbers on all models to help cure an inherent wheel hop problem that had required the installation of a single traction control bar on the right rear corner of 1967 models with certain performance-oriented powertrain combinations. Combining the staggered shocks with new multiple-leaf rear springs beneath 1968 Camaro Super Sports did away with the need for a traction bar installation.

Exterior changes were minor. Vent windows were deleted, and government-mandated side marker lights were added. The Rally Sport package returned and once more could be combined with Super Sport equipment to make for one way-cool Camaro. SS touches carried over in similar fashion, with the most notable difference involving the SS 396's new simulated hood vents, which contained four equally fake carburetor stacks. The 1968 SS 350's vents were the same as those seen the previous year on all Camaro Super Sport hoods.

The Super Sport's bumblebee striping (listed separately as RPO D91) up front made an encore appearance, but this time buyers could supersede the bumblebee pattern by a new set of stripes that ran over the nose and turned backward down the bodysides, ending near the doors' trailing edges.

1968 CAMARO SS

Model availability	2-door sport coupe, 2-door convertible
Wheelbase	108 inches
Length	184.7 inches
Width	72.5 inches
Height	51.4 inches
Curb weight	3,855 pounds (SS 396 coupe)
Price	RPO L48 cost $210.65, RPO L35 cost $263.30, RPO L34 cost $368.65, RPO L78 cost $500.30, RPO L89 cost $868.95 (base V-8 coupe: $2,670; base V-8 convertible: $2,908)
Track	59/58.9 (front/rear, in inches)
Wheels	14 × 6 stamped-steel
Tires	F70 × 14
Suspension	independent unequal A-arms, coil springs & stabilizer bar in front; multi-leaf springs, solid axle w/staggered shocks in back
Steering	recirculating ball
Brakes	hydraulic drums, front & rear
Engine	290-horsepower 350-cubic-inch L48 V-8, 325-horsepower 396-cubic-inch L35 V-8, 350-horsepower 306-cubic-inch L34 V-8, 375-horsepower 396-cubic-inch L78 V-8, 375-horsepower aluminum-head 396-cubic-inch L89 V-8
Bore & stroke	4.00 × 3.48 inches, 350 V-8; 4.094 × 3.76 inches, 396 V-8
Compression	10.25:1 (L48, L34 & L35 V-8s), 11:1 (L78 & L89 V-8)
Fuel delivery	single 4-barrel carburetor
Transmission	3-speed manual std. w/350 V-8; special 3-speed std. w/396 V-8

Above: The SS 396 Camaro was available in three flavors in 1968 as a 350-horsepower L34 Turbo Jet big-block joined the rollover L35 and L78 Mk IV V-8 engines. An aluminum-head option (RPO L89) also appeared for the solid-lifter L78. A black cove panel in back denoted the Turbo Jet's presence up front.

Right: Big-block Super Sport hoods in 1968 received unique simulated vents featuring four fake carburetor stacks in each.

Opposite: In 1969, the Camaro SS was made even more attractive by a restyled nose and the new ZL2 cowl induction hood. *GM*

Optional fiberglass front and rear spoilers (D80) also appeared midyear.

Super Sport drivetrains rolled over with one new addition, as the 350-horsepower L35 396 joined its L34 and L78 big-block brothers. Limited to the L34 only in 1967, the Turbo Hydra-Matic automatic transmission was made available as well behind the L35 in 1968, as was a four-speed manual. Weight-saving aluminum heads (RPO L89) debuted, but their heavy price tag ($868.95) inhibited their popularity. Only 272 sets were sold.

1969

Camaro was treated to a major facelift for its third edition, and most critics still agree the change was for the better in a big way. Looking more aggressive all around, 1969's Super Sport appeared even hotter when topped off in front with the new ZL2 cowl induction hood, a fully functional unit designed by Larry Shinoda. Priced at $79, this lid was limited to SS, Z28, and COPO applications. Total ZL2 production for 1969 was 10,026. New,

too, was an optional body-colored Endura front bumper (RPO VE3), a $42.15 option that attracted 12,650 buyers that year.

The Rally Sport package carried over in similar fashion for 1969, but the Super Sport deal was restructured. Listed as RPO Z27, it included a 300-horsepower 350 small-block backed by a three-speed stick, special suspension, F70 Wide Oval rubber on 14 × 7 wheels, power front disc brakes, a unique hood, sport striping, and familiar SS identification, all priced rather nicely at $295.95.

1969 CAMARO SS

Model availability	2-door sport coupe, 2-door convertible
Wheelbase	108 inches
Length	186 inches
Width	74 inches
Height	51.6 inches, coupe; 51.5 inches, convertible
Curb weight	3,490 pounds (SS 396 coupe)
Price	RPO Z27 (Super Sport Package w/base 350 V-8) cost $295.95, L35 V-8 added $63.20, L34 V-8 added $184.35, L78 V-8 added $316, L89 V-8 added $710.95 (base V-8 coupe: $2,727; base V-8 convertible: $2,940)
Track	59.6/59.5 (front/rear, in inches)
Wheels	14 × 7
Tires	F70 Wide Oval w/raised white letters
Suspension	independent unequal A-arms, coil springs & stabilizer bar in front; multi-leaf springs, solid axle w/staggered shocks in back
Steering	recirculating ball
Brakes	power front discs, rear drums
Engine	300-horsepower 350-cubic-inch L48 V-8, 325-horsepower 396-cubic-inch L35 V-8, 350-horsepower 396-cubic-inch L34 V-8, 375-horsepower 39-cubic-inch L78 V-8, 375-horsepower aluminum-head 396-cubic-inch L89 V-8
Bore & stroke	4.00 × 3.48 inches, 350 V-8; 4.094 × 3.76 inches, 396 V-8
Compression	10.25:1 (L48 & L35 V-8s), 11:1 (L78 V-8)
Fuel delivery	single 4-barrel carburetor
Transmission	3-speed manual std. w/L48; special 3-speed std. w/L35 & L78

Creating a Camaro SS 396 was typically a matter of replacing the Z27 group's 350 V-8 with one of the same four optional big-blocks listed in 1968. The aluminum-head L89/L78 combo was a rare installation once more: only 311 were made in 1969. Even fewer and farther between was the JL8 power-assisted four-wheel disc option, priced at $500.30. Only 206 JL8 applications are known for 1969 Camaros.

Last but certainly not least, a Camaro SS was chosen to pace the Indianapolis 500 for the second time in 1969. In 1967, a blue-striped, white-painted SS/RS convertible had led the field around the Brickyard, and Chevrolet followed that up by manufacturing an unknown number of pace car replicas, all colored similarly with either 350 small-block or 396 big-block V-8s. Two years later, a fully documented run of Indy pace car replicas appeared, officially listed under RPO Z11.

Opposite: In 1969, Chevrolet marked the Camaro's second appearance as the Indianapolis 500 pace car with a run of replicas, officially listed under RPO Z11. Z11 production was 3,675.

Below left: As in 1967, 1969's Indy pace car Camaros were fitted with both 350 small-block and 396 big-block engines. The actual pace car used a 375-horsepower L78 396, shown here.

Below right: Power front disc brakes were standard for the Super Sport Camaro in 1969.

All 3,675 of these were SS/RS convertibles done in Dover White paint with Hugger Orange stripes and orange houndstooth interiors. Rally wheels and cowl induction hoods were included in all cases too.

A similarly adorned pace car replica coupe appeared with many of the same features, including both Super Sport and Rally Sport equipment. A promotional package created for Chevrolet's Southwestern Branch Zone Office, this option was tabbed Z10.

1969 COPO

Like Chevelle, Camaro was limited to no more than 400 cubes worth of engine prior to 1970. But again, that rule didn't stop Vince Piggins, who once more worked his COPO magic in 1969. Two 427-powered Camaro models appeared that year thanks to Piggins and a little help from a pair of quick-thinking Chevy dealers.

In Pennsylvania, Yenko Chevrolet had been transforming SS 396 pony cars into Corvette-powered screamers for two years by the time

Above: Only sixty-nine COPO 9560 ZL-1 Camaros were built in 1969: twenty-two with automatic transmissions, forty-seven with four-speeds.

Opposite top: All Z11 Indy pace car replica convertibles in 1969 were painted Dover White with orange stripes complemented with orange hound's-tooth interiors.

Opposite bottom: Various delays pushed the revamped Camaro's introduction back to February 1970, meaning the 1969 models carried over unchanged early in the year—as the license plate on this press release photo attests. *GM*

Don Yenko met with Chevy officials in the summer of 1968 to discuss the possibility of a factory-built 427 Camaro, a package that would save him the trouble of making further engine swaps. Piggins's response was COPO number 9561, which specified the assembly-line installation of the Corvette's L72 427 big-block into a special run of 1969 Camaros.

Rated at 425 horsepower, the L72 featured 11:1 compression, a lumpy solid-lifter cam, closed-chamber heads, and a big 780-cfm Holley four-barrel on an aluminum dual-plane intake. The ZL2 hood, a heavy-duty Harrison radiator, heavy-duty springs, and a beefed-up Positraction rear with 4.10:1 gears were also included in the COPO 9561 deal. Optional 4.56:1 cogs were offered, and a buyer could opt for a four-speed or automatic.

The production count for COPO 9561 is not known. Chevrolet's Tonawanda engine plant reportedly turned out 1,015 L72 427s (193 automatics, 822 manuals) for F-body installations in 1969, but how many of those actually went into Camaros sold to the public is undocumented. The first hundred L72 Camaros went to Yenko that year, and at least another hundred followed later, all to be decked out in Yenko S/C striping. Berger Chevrolet in Michigan also reportedly took delivery of fifty COPO Camaros for its own special promotion.

1969 COPO CAMARO

Model availability	2-door sport coupe
Wheelbase	108 inches
Length	186 inches
Width	74 inches
Height	51.6 inches
Weight	3,300 pounds (COPO 9560)
Price	COPO 9561 cost $489.45. COPO 9560 cost $4,160
Track	59.6/59.5 (front/rear, in inches)
Wheels	14 × 7
Tires	F70 Wide Oval w/raised white letters
Suspension	independent unequal A-arms, heavy-duty coil springs & stabilizer bar in front; heavy-duty leaf springs, solid axle w/staggered shocks in back
Steering	recirculating ball
Brakes	power front discs, rear drums
Engine	425-horsepower 427-cubic-inch cast-iron L72 V-8 (COPO 9561), 430-horsepower 427-cubic-inch all-aluminum ZL1 V-8 (COPO 9560)
Bore & stroke	4.25 × 3.76 inches
Compression	11:1 (L72), 12:1 (ZL-1)
Fuel delivery	780-cfm Holley 4-barrel carburetor (L72), 850-cfm Holley double-pumper 4-barrel carburetor (ZL-1)
Transmission	4-speed manual or heavy-duty Turbo Hydra-Matic automatic
Axle ratio	4.10:1 Positraction in heavy-duty 12-bolt housing

Above: The 427-cubic-inch ZL-1 V-8's cylinder block and heads were all made of aluminum. Output was a token-rated 430 horsepower. Compression was 12:1.

Opposite: A twelve-bolt rear end containing 4.10:1 Positraction gears was standard for the ZL-1 Camaro in 1969.

1969 ZL1 Camaro Production Breakdown

	Gibb Chevrolet		Other Dealerships	
Paint	TH400	4-speed	TH400	4-speed
Hugger Orange	4	6	1	5
Lemans Blue	4	6	1	2
Cortez Silver	4	6	0	2
Fathom Green	4	6	0	2
Dusk Blue	4	6	0	0
Daytona Yellow	0	0	0	2
Dover White	0	0	0	2
Garnet Red	0	0	0	2
Total: 69	**20**	**30**	**2**	**17**

No mystery whatsoever surrounds the second COPO F-body created in 1969. Essentially every nut and bolt on the famed ZL-1 Camaro has been fingerprinted and filed away for posterity. Exactly sixty-nine of these big-block beasts were built (twenty-two with automatics, forty-seven with four-speeds) using COPO number 9560, and all were clearly meant for racing duty only.

Unlike the comparatively tame L72, the ZL-1 427 plain and simply wasn't suited for civilized operation. Its beefed-up block (with cast-iron cylinder sleeves) and race-ready open-chamber heads were cast in weight-saving aluminum, as was its cavernous open-plenum intake and bell housing. A huge 850-cfm Holley double-pumper sat atop that intake, just the monster needed

to keep the air fuel flowing through the ZL-1's big valves and large round ports. A truly radical mechanical cam bumped those valves, and compression was a severe 12:1. Though Chevrolet laughingly rated the aluminum 427 at 430 horsepower, actual output easily soared past 500 horses at a dizzying seven thousand revolutions per minute.

Magazine road testers in 1969 wasted little time making a mockery of that token 430-horse tag. *Cars* testers managed a 13.16-second, 110.21-mile-per-hour quarter-mile pass in a four-speed ZL-1 Camaro right out of the box. Veteran racer Dick Harrell added headers (with full exhausts) and slicks to an automatic ZL-1 and produced an 11.85/119.06 run for *Super Stock*

magazine. Uncapping the headers resulted in an 11.64/122.15 time slip, and later tests pushed the outside of the envelope even further into the mid-teens. In 1971, a Pro Stock ZL-1 Camaro using twin Holley Dominator carbs set an AHRA record of 9.63 seconds at 143 miles per hour.

It was Dick Harrell, working in concert with Illinois Chevrolet dealer Fred Gibb, who inspired the ZL-1

Above: The COPO 9561 engine was the Corvette's L72 427 big-block, rated at 425 horsepower. The cylinder block and closed-chamber heads were cast iron. The carburetor was a 780-cfm Holley four-barrel.

Opposite: Save for the standard ZL-2 hood, almost nothing revealed the identity of an L72 Camaro in 1969. This COPO 9561 car is fitted with optional spoilers in the front and rear.

Above: COPO cars were used by Yenko Chevrolet to create a special run of Yenko S/C Camaros in 1969.

Opposite top: In garden-variety COPO applications, the Corvette's L72 V-8 was rated at 425 horsepower. Yenko Chevrolet upped the advertised ante to 450 horses when they converted a COPO Camaro into a Yenko Super Car in 1969.

Opposite bottom: Pure paradox—Chevrolet's air injection reactor system was required in 1969, even on the high-performance L72 427, shown here. The race-ready ZL-1 also got this plumbing, although it didn't use it for long in 1969.

Camaro's creation. Like Yenko, Gibb and Harrell approached Piggins in 1968 with a request to use COPO paperwork to build 427 Camaros, both L72s and ZL-1s. NHRA drag racing rules then specified that at least fifty examples of a particular production car be built to legalize that vehicle for stock class competition. Again, no problem. Gibb ordered fifty COPO 9560 Camaros for his lot in LaHarpe, Illinois, with the first two arriving on New Year's Day 1969. Another nineteen cars were built and went to various dealers across the country. These dealers, like Gibb, quickly found out how tough it was to market this high-strung, high-priced Camaro.

Base price for a typical V-8 Camaro in 1969 was $2,727. COPO 9560 tacked on another $4,160.15, or just about the amount Gibb figured the entire car would cost. An official price was still

in the works when he placed his order; he guessed that $4,900 would be tops. Nearly all the cars had arrived in Illinois before GM sent the bill in March. A bit overwhelmed, he somehow managed to send twenty ZL-1s back to the Norwood, Ohio, plant, where they were reluctantly redistributed.

The COPO 9560 package included the ZL-1 427, ZL2 hood, Harrison radiator, transistorized ignition, heavy-duty suspension, and the equally tough twelve-bolt Posi-Traction rear end with 4.10:1 gears. Boosting the bottom line further were a few mandatory options: power front discs and either a Muncie M21 close-ratio four-speed or a Turbo Hydra-Matic 400 auto box, both with aluminum cases. Chevy's mean-and-nasty M22 Rock Crusher four-speed was available at extra cost, as were those loud, cackling, chambered exhausts.

1970

Pony car watchers eagerly awaited a veritable rebirth for GM's F-body in the fall of 1969. Hank Haga's styling studio had been busy fashioning a new and improved Camaro dating back to late 1966, and the word just couldn't help but get out. But when Chevrolet's new models were announced in September, a 1970 Camaro failed to appear. Various glitches, combined with designers' desires to unveil no new F-body before its time, worked in concert to delay its introduction. Buyers initially were told to take 1969 leftovers and like it.

Meanwhile, GM execs continued teasing the pony car–buying public. "We will give an entirely new direction to this market," claimed Chevrolet general manager John DeLorean in a January 1970 *Motor Trend* interview. Chevy's upcoming new Camaro, in his words, would be "so sensational that I think we will more than make up for lost ground."

Indeed, almost all was forgiven when a totally fresh Camaro finally emerged in February 1970. Low, long, and wide, this sleek machine was commonly praised for the way its expensive-looking facade and markedly upgraded feel masked its affordable, compact nature. According

1970½ CAMARO SS

Model availability	2-door sport coupe
Wheelbase	108 inches
Length	188 inches
Width	74.4 inches
Height	50.5 inches
Curb weight	3,670 pounds (w/base 350 V-8)
Price	RPO Z27 (Super Sport Package w/base 350 V-8) cost $289.65, L34 V-8 added $152.75, L78 V-8 added $385.50 (base V-8 coupe: $2,839)
Track	61.3/60 (front/rear, in inches)
Wheels	14 × 7
Tires	F70 Wide Oval w/raised white letters
Suspension	independent unequal A-arms, coil springs & stabilizer bar in front; multi-leaf springs, solid axle w/staggered shocks in back
Steering	recirculating ball
Brakes	power front discs, rear drums
Engine	300-horsepower 350-cubic-inch L48 V-8, 350-horsepower 402-cubic-inch L34 V-8, 375-horsepower 402 cubic-inch L78 V-8
Bore & stroke	4.00 × 3.48 inches, 350 V-8; 4.126 × 3.76 inches, 402 V-8
Compression	10.25:1 (L48 & L34 V-8s), 11:1 (L78 V-8)
Fuel delivery	single 4-barrel carburetor
Transmission	4-speed manual or Turbo Hydra-Matic automatic

Left: This preproduction mockup shows the small, individual bumpers that would be included as part of 1970's Rally Sport package.

Opposite: Reminiscent of Chevrolet's classic two-door Nomad station wagons of 1955 to 1957, the Kammback concept was originally crafted on a first-generation Camaro platform. The idea was further developed for the next-generation F-body planned for 1970.

Below: A full-width bumper was standard for the Camaro SS in 1970.

to *Detroit News* columnist Bob Irvin, the so-called 1970½ Camaro was "a beautiful looking automobile, one that makes the Mustang and Barracuda seem like last year's models." Warmly welcomed updates beneath its sexy skin included standard front disc brakes.

Though a convertible wasn't offered, the Super Sport and Rally Sport renditions remained. Still tabbed Z27, the SS package featured power brakes, special trim, F70 tires on 14 × 7 wheels, a black-painted grille, and hideaway windshield wipers. The 350 small-block remained the base V-8 and produced 300 horsepower. Optional engines

included the L34 and L78 big-blocks, once more rated at 350 and 375 horsepower, respectively. Both were labeled 396 Turbo-Jet V-8s even though a slight bore job had increased actual displacement to 402 cubic inches. Transmission choices included a wide- or close-ratio four-speed or the TH400 automatic.

Less prominent without its hideaway headlights, the Z22 Rally Sport group was quickly identified by the two small bumpers found up front in place of the standard Camaro's full-width unit. Bright accents and blackout treatments completed the deal.

1971

Only minor changes marked the 1971 Camaro's arrival, and the Super Sport and Rally Sport versions rolled over essentially unchanged. Most notable were power cutbacks for both the base 350 and the optional LS3 402 big-block, as compression cuts (down to 8.5:1) were made across the board.

1971 CAMARO SS

Model availability	2-door sport coupe
Wheelbase	108 inches
Length	188 inches
Width	74.4 inches
Height	50.5 inches
Weight	3,810 pounds (SS 396)
Price	RPO Z27 (Super Sport Package w/base 350 V-8) cost $313.90, LS3 V-8 added $99.05 (base V-8 coupe: $2,848)
Track	61.3/60 (front/rear, in inches)
Wheels	14 × 7
Tires	F70 Wide Oval w/raised white letters
Suspension	independent unequal A-arms, coil springs & stabilizer bar in front; multi-leaf springs, solid axle w/staggered shocks in back
Steering	recirculating ball
Brakes	power front discs, rear drums
Engine	270-horsepower 350-cubic-inch L48 V-8, 300-horsepower 402-cubic-inch LS3 V-8
Bore & stroke	4.00 × 3.48 inches, 350 V-8; 4.126 × 3.76 inches, 402 V-8
Compression	8.5:1
Fuel delivery	single 4-barrel carburetor
Transmission	4-speed manual or Turbo Hydra-Matic automatic

Opposite top: Only six hundred L78 Super Sport Camaros were built for 1970, the last year for the supreme 396 Turbo Jet. *Tom Shaw*

Opposite bottom: Both the SS and RS packages rolled on basically unchanged for 1971. The Rally Sport shown here was powered by the L48 350 small-block, now rated at 270 horsepower.

Below: Road & Track named Chevrolet's Camaro SS 350 one of the world's ten best cars in 1971.

1972

The Camaro Super Sport rolled out for one more year before succumbing to sagging popularity. Power again fell off in 1972, as the base L48 350 was net-rated at 200 horses, the LS3 Turbo-Jet at 240. In the Super Sport's place for 1973 was the new Type LT Camaro, offered as an individual model with a V-8 only.

Opposite Chevrolet superseded its Super Sport Camaro in 1973 with the Type LT.

Below: Only two engines were available for the last Camaro SS in 1972: the base L48 350 and optional LS3 big-block.

1972 CAMARO SS

Model availability	2-door sport coupe
Wheelbase	108 inches
Length	188 inches
Width	74.4 inches
Height	50.5 inches
Price	RPO Z27 (Super Sport Package w/base 350 V-8) cost $306.35, LS3 V-8 added $96 (base V-8 coupe: $2,819.70)
Track	61.3/60 (front/rear, in inches)
Wheels	14 × 7
Tires	F70 Wide Oval w/raised white letters
Suspension	independent unequal A-arms, coil springs & stabilizer bar in front; multi-leaf springs, solid axle w/ staggered shocks in back
Steering	recirculating ball
Brakes	power front discs, rear drums
Engine	200-horsepower 350-cubic-inch L48 V-8, 240-horsepower 402-cubic-inch LS3 V-8
Bore & stroke	4.00 × 3.48 inches, 350 V-8; 4.126 × 3.76 inches, 402 V-8
Compression	8.5:1
Fuel delivery	single 4-barrel carburetor
Transmission	4-speed manual or Turbo Hydra-Matic automatic

1967–1972 Camaro Super Sport Production Figures

	L48	L35	L34	LS3	L78	L89[1]	Total
1967	29,270	4,003	n/a	n/a	1,138	n/a	34,411
1968	12,496	10,773	2,579	n/a	4,575	272	30,695
1969	22,339	6,752	2,018	n/a	4,889	311	34,932
1970	10,012	n/a	1,864	n/a	600	n/a	12,476
1971	6,844	n/a	n/a	1,533	n/a	n/a	8,377
1972	5,592	n/a	n/a	970	n/a	n/a	6,562

NOTE: Eagle-eyes may notice that 1969's engine count (36,309) does not match that year's total Z27 Super Sport tally. According to various sources (including the Camaro Research Group), this discrepancy (1,377 more engines than cars) may well be the result of 1969's COPO build, as these 427-equipped Camaros began life as L78 SS models but were released with no SS identification. Hence, 1969's COPO Camaro count may be hiding within those 4,889 L78 cars.
[1] Aluminum head option for L78

TRANS-AM TERROR

David Kimble

Camaro Z28: 1967–1974

The game was called homologation, a derivative of the Greek *homologos*, roughly meaning "in agreement." Homologation was the process by which a competition version of a regular-production automobile was legalized for on-track duty during stock class racing's heyday back in the 1960s. In most cases, a minimum production standard was the main homologating standard: a company had to build so many street-going examples of a certain car to qualify said machine for a certain racing class. Technical specifications also entered into the equation.

▶ Original press reports of the Trans-Am Camaro used the RPO list reference: Z-28. Badges that showed up in 1968 then morph the tag into Z/28. The name later became simply Z28, which appears on these pages in the best interests of consistency.

▶ All first-, second-, and third-generation Z28s were coupes.

▶ Ford's Trans-Am pony car, the Boss 302 Mustang, debuted for 1969.

▶ Another rival, Pontiac's aptly named Trans Am, also debuted for 1969.

▶ Dodge's T/A Challenger and Plymouth's AAR 'Cuda joined the Trans-Am series in 1970.

▶ New SCCA rules allowing destroked production engines made it possible to install the Corvette's 350-cubic-inch LT-1 V-8 into the revamped 1970½ Z28.

▶ Temporarily shelved after 1974, Z28 reappeared midyear in 1977.

▶ One mysterious Z28 was built for 1975.

In the case of the Sports Car Club of America's (SCCA) Trans American Sedan Championship, opened for business in March 1966, the most important qualification early on involved engine displacement. Soon known simply as Trans-Am racing, this stock class league at first was broken up into two groups, one for compacts with engines displacing less than 2 liters, the other for sedans carrying more than 2 liters worth of powerplant. Capping the O-2 (over 2 liters) class was a displacement limit of 5 liters, or about 305 cubic inches. Additional specifications also eventually included a minimum run of one thousand cars built for public sale.

Ford's Mustang, with its 289-cubic-inch V-8, qualified easily and led the way during Trans-Am racing's first two seasons, beating up mostly on a bunch of Plymouth Barracudas and Dodge Darts in 1966. Hitting the road again the following year almost didn't happen, though, as next to no one—except for Ford fans—apparently was interested in watching a one-horse show. Fortunately, additional factory involvement was announced not long after the seven-race 1966 season ended, ensuring at least an encore for Trans-Am competition.

Twelve events followed in 1967, the year both Mercury and Chevrolet joined the fray full force. From there the race was truly on, as American Motors, Dodge, and Plymouth all took to SCCA racing before the bubble burst three years later. With *horsepower* soon a dirty word around Detroit, all but AMC cancelled their direct support of Trans-Am teams between October 1970 and April 1971. The league itself, in its briefly legendary original form, was history by the end of 1972.

But hold your horses: weren't GM's divisions all restricted from direct racing involvement per that infamous executive decree sent down in 1963? Certainly. But just as Chevrolet engineers had kept the back door open to preferred racers after the 1957 AMA ban on factory racing involvement, so too did certain movers and shakers following GM's own in-house edict six years later. Among those who circumvented the rules more than once during the 1960s was ever-present COPO-man Vince Piggins.

An assistant staff engineer in charge of product promotion in 1966, Piggins was no stranger to a racetrack. The famed NASCAR champion Hudson Hornets of the early 1950s had been his babies. And after Chevrolet took to stock car racing seriously in 1955, he was brought on board the next year to oversee the company's clandestine competition program. In between that time and 1969, when Piggins shepherded those 427-powered Chevelles and Camaros through the COPO loophole, he was also responsible for the hot little pony car that helped vault the Trans-Am series into the limelight.

Above: Familiar Z/28 badges didn't appear until midyear 1968. *Jeremy Cliff photo, courtesy Mecum Auctions*

Previous pages: Left: All 1967 Z28 Camaros were coupes with four-speed manual transmissions. Very rare Evening Orchid paint (a 1965 Chevy shade) was special ordered for this model, originally sold by Grabiak Chevrolet in New Alexandria, Pennsylvania. *courtesy Mecum Auctions Right:* Engineers created the Z28's 302 V-8 by stuffing a 283 crank into a 327 block. That block in 1967 and 1968 featured mundane two-bolt main bearing caps. Four-bolt mains appeared in 1969. *David Kimble cutaway, courtesy GM*

Opposite: Except for standard Rally wheels, racing stripes on the hood and the deck lid made up the only outward clues as to a Z28's presence in 1967.

On August 17, 1966, Piggins issued a memo to Chevrolet brass outlining his plan to build an SCCA-legal Camaro, a car possessing "performance and handling characteristics superior to either Mustang or Barracuda." Once approved, Piggins's proposed package was given RPO Z28, a simply stark label that stuck despite Piggins's pleas for the name "Cheetah."

To meet SCCA homologation standards, the Z28 had to have a back seat (which made it a sedan), a wheelbase no longer than 116 inches, and, as mentioned, an engine no larger than 305 cubic inches. Too bad the smallest thing then in the Camaro arsenal was the 327 V-8. Original experiments with a high-performance version of the good ol' 283 small-block proved

acceptable, but Piggins wanted to exploit every inch he could get his mitts on. He managed to up the displacement ante to 302 by simply bolting a 283 crank into a 327 block, resulting in a mighty mouse motor that made plenty of ponies, 290 on paper.

In the real world, that advertised number fooled almost no one. "The 290-hp figure quoted for the Z-28 engine seems ridiculously conservative," noted a *Car and Driver* claim. "It feels at least as strong as the 327, 350-hp engine offered in the Corvette." According to *Sports Car Graphic*'s Jerry Titus, it was "logical to expect a fully prepared version [of the 302] to produce well in excess of 370 honest ponies." Reportedly, the speed merchants at Traco Engineering coaxed more than

500 horsepower from the 302s they built for Roger Penske's Trans-Am race team.

Although Piggins initially projected a run of at least 10,000 Camaro Z28s for 1967, the actual count was only a mere 602. But it was a start. Though rarely seen at first, Detroit's original Trans-Am pony car was hard to overlook on the street scene. "With the Z-28, Chevy is on the way toward making the gutsy stormer the Camaro should have been in the first place," proclaimed a *Car and Driver* review. Trackside witnesses also were impressed, as Camaro Z28s dominated Trans-Am racing in 1968 and 1969, results that in turn helped sales soar.

The Z28 temporarily retired after 1974, then returned triumphantly three years later.

Above: Corvette-style 15-inch Rally wheels were standard in 1967. These rims differed slightly in offset compared to their Sting Ray–targeted counterparts.

Opposite: Standard Z28 tires in 1967 were 7.35x15 units adorned with either red or white stripes.

Right: Optional cowl induction ductwork was delivered inside a Z28's trunk in 1967. Adding this air cleaner upped the Z28 package's price from $358.10 to $437.10.

1967 CAMARO Z28

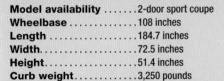

Model availability	2-door sport coupe
Wheelbase	108 inches
Length	184.7 inches
Width	72.5 inches
Height	51.4 inches
Curb weight	3,250 pounds
Base price	$3,226
Track	59/58.9 (front/rear, in inches)
Wheels	15 × 6 Rally rims
Tires	7.35 × 15 red-stripe
Suspension	independent A-arms, coil springs & stabilizer bar in front; solid axle w/single-leaf springs & right side trailing link in back
Steering	recirculating ball
Brakes	power-assisted front discs, rear drums
Engine	290-horsepower 302-cubic-inch V-8
Bore & stroke	4.00 × 3.00 inches
Compression	11:1
Fuel delivery	800-cfm Holley 4-barrel carburetor on aluminum high-rise intake manifold
Transmission	close-ratio M21 4-speed w/Muncie shifter
Axle ratio	3.73:1

1967

Introduced to the automotive press on November 26, 1966, at Riverside, California, the first Camaro Z28 truly was a well-rounded performer. Along with its exclusive 302-cubic-inch small-block, the package included Chevrolet's superb F41 suspension, a quick-ratio Saginaw manual steering box, and 3.73:1 rear gears. A Muncie four-speed (with 2.20:1 low) was a mandatory option (no automatics were allowed either), as were front disc brakes with power-assist. Thrown in along with those discs were four 15 × 6 Corvette-type Rally wheels. Other than these bright rims, the only other outward clues to a '67 Z28's presence were twin racing stripes on the hood and rear deck. The legendary Z/28 emblem didn't debut until midway through 1968.

Popular options included a fiberglass rear spoiler and the Z22 Rally Sport group. The sky was the limit from there, as all available Camaro frills—save for SS equipment and air conditioning—were available along with RPO Z28, but only for a V-8 coupe. No convertibles were allowed.

Among options exclusive to the Z28 application were tube headers and a fresh-air induction setup. This special air cleaner came boxed in the trunk

and featured ductwork that ran from the carburetor to a plenum in the cowl. Ordering RPO Z28 with the dealer-installed headers required shelling out an extra $779.40 in 1967. On its own, the Z28 option cost $358.10. The price was $437.10 with the cowl induction equipment and a whopping $858.40 with both the fresh-air ducting and the headers.

As for the heart of this beast, the 290-horse 302 small-block was hot to trot from top to bottom. Though the cylinder block was a typical passenger-car unit with two-bolt main bearings (stronger four-bolt mains came along in 1969), the rugged crank was made of forged steel instead of nodular cast iron. Below that crank went a windage tray to prevent oil sloshing in the pan during hard turns or serious acceleration. On top were L79 big-valve (2.02-inch intakes, 1.60 exhausts) heads and an 800-cfm Holley four-barrel carburetor on an aluminum intake. Compression was 11:1. Along with various chrome dress-up pieces, the 302 V-8 also was treated to deep-groove pulleys, transistorized ignition, a heavy-duty radiator, and a five-blade viscous-drive fan.

Transmission choices numbered two: the M20 wide-ratio four-speed or its M21 close-ratio running mate, both priced at $184.35.

Yet another rare dealer-installed option also broke corporate rules. Supposedly, multiple-carb setups were taboo after 1966 in all GM models save for Corvette, but leave it to Piggins to promote a cross-ram aluminum intake mounting two Holley four-barrels for the Z28's 302 V-8. The price for this race-ready service part was about $500. It was offered through 1969.

Above: Adding the custom interior option (RPO Z87) into the Z28 mix in 1967 required spending an extra $94.80. Included in the Z87 deal were molded front armrests, a deluxe steering wheel, and color-keyed accents on the seats.

Right: A hungry Holley four-barrel on an aluminum intake delivered air/fuel to the Z28's 302-cubic-inch small-block V-8. Heads were big-port L79 units.

Opposite: After appearing rather clandestinely in 1967, the Z28 was promoted rather prominently in magazine ads the following year. *Jeremy Cliff photo, courtesy Mecum Auctions*

1968

Basically the same package rolled over for 1968, with minor updates including switching from single-leaf springs to four-leaf units with staggered shock absorbers in back. New, larger center caps graced this year's Rally wheels, shod in Goodyear Wide Tread GT E70 tires. New, too, was a third transmission choice, the gnarly M22 Rock Crusher four-speed, priced at an equally mean and nasty $310.70.

Price changes also made news in 1968, as the RPO Z28 tag increased to $400.25. Adding the plenum air cleaner into the mix bumped that number up to $479.25, but the super rare headers cost the same as in 1967. Another dealer-installed option—four-wheel disc brakes—showed up in 1968, this after Trans-Am race teams demonstrated the brakes' merits on SCCA road courses. Few of these brake packages were sold over dealership parts counters, and the option then became officially listed on the Camaro RPO list as JL8 in 1969.

1968 CAMARO Z28

Model availability	2-door sport coupe
Wheelbase	108 inches
Length	184.7 inches
Width	72.5 inches
Height	51.4 inches
Curb weight	3,250 pounds
Base price	$3,256
Track	59/58.9 (front/rear, in inches)
Wheels	15 × 6 Rally rims
Tires	E70 Goodyear Wide Tread GT w/raised white letters
Suspension	independent A-arms, coil springs & stabilizer bar in front; solid axle w/multi-leaf springs & staggered shock absorbers in back
Steering	recirculating ball
Brakes	power-assisted front discs, rear drums
Engine	290-horsepower 302-cubic-inch V-8
Bore & stroke	4.00 × 3.00 inches
Compression	11:1
Fuel delivery	800-cfm Holley 4-barrel carburetor on aluminum high-rise intake manifold
Transmission	close-ratio M21 4-speed w/Muncie shifter
Axle ratio	3.73:1

1969 CAMARO Z28

Model availability	2-door sport coupe
Wheelbase	108 inches
Length	186 inches
Width	74 inches
Height	51.6 inches
Curb weight	3,455 pounds
Base price	$3,266
Track	59.6/59.5 (front/rear, in inches)
Wheels	15 × 7 Rally rims
Tires	E70 × 15
Suspension	independent A-arms, coil springs & stabilizer bar in front; solid axle w/multi-leaf springs & staggered shock absorbers in back
Steering	recirculating ball
Brakes	power-assisted front discs, rear drums (4-wheel discs, optional)
Engine	290-horsepower 302-cubic-inch V-8
Bore & stroke	4.00 × 3.00 inches
Compression	11:1
Fuel delivery	800-cfm Holley 4-barrel carburetor on high-rise aluminum intake manifold
Transmission	close-ratio M21 4-speed w/Hurst shifter
Axle ratio	3.73:1

1969

Chevrolet's nicely restyled 1969 Camaro body suited the Z28 to a T, even more so when topped off by the functional ZL2 hood with its rear-facing scoop, introduced on November 25, 1968. Nearly all standard features carried over unchanged, and the Rally Sport package was again available, featuring prominently styled headlight doors. The rarely seen JL8 four-wheel-disc package was a $500.30 option.

Notable upgrades included a more durable 302-cylinder block refitted with four-bolt main bearing caps, a thicker front stabilizer bar, and wider 15 × 7 wheels, although some early models apparently used 1968's 15 × 6 rims. Two different tires were installed in 1969: the E70 Goodyear Wide Tread GT was joined by Firestone's Sport Car 200. New, too, was a more precise, definitely preferred Hurst shifter in place of the clunky Muncie stick used in 1967 and 1968.

Various changes were made to the Z28 equipment group during the year, as more than one individual component came and went. Low-restriction, chambered exhausts were briefly included in RPO Z28, as were a tachometer, rear deck spoiler, and chrome exhaust tips. Prices ranged from $485.15 to $522.40. One little-known variation involved deleting the stripes on the hood and deck lid.

Left: The Z28's V-8 featured various upgrades in 1969, not the least of which was a more durable cylinder block with four-bolt main bearing caps. Advertised output remained at a conservative 290 horsepower.

Opposite top: New 15 × 7 Rally wheels featuring enlarged center caps were standard for the restyled Z28 in 1969.

Opposite bottom: A rear spoiler was optional in 1969.

Right: The Z28's V-8 featured various upgrades in 1969, not the least of which was a more durable cylinder block with four-bolt main bearing caps. Advertised output remained at a conservative 290 horsepower.

Opposite top: A cross-ram intake featuring two Holley four-barrels was offered over dealer counters as a service package option for the Z28 from 1967 to 1969. *courtesy Mecum Auctions*

Opposite bottom: Z28 Camaros were SCCA Trans-Am champions in 1968 and 1969, thanks in part to the work of the Penske-Sunoco team. *GM*

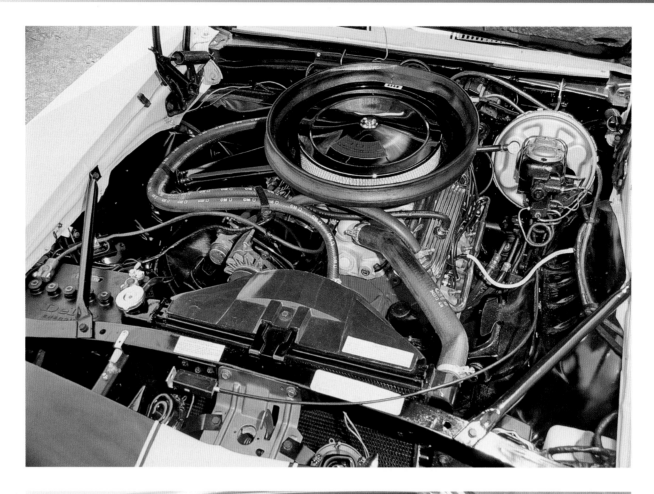

Chevrolet's unforgettable hounds-tooth interior was available in four shades in 1969: ivory, yellow, black, and orange, the latter used for that year's Indy 500 pace car replicas.

1970½

Another excitingly new Z28 emerged along with Chevrolet's redesigned 1970½ Camaro to take the legacy to even greater heights. "It's quiet, quick, beautiful, and all the parts look and act as though they belong together," claimed *Sports Car Graphic*'s Paul Van Valkenburgh in reference to the fourth-edition Z.

Next to the cranky, hot-tempered 1969 Z28 with its loud, skittish, rough-idling 302 small-block, the next-gen model was a kinder, gentler machine, a still-strong performer that *Car Life* claimed was "as close to a mild-mannered racing car as the industry has come." Real men who preferred a real racer complete with a real racer's really bad nature preferred the original Trans-Am pony car, as rough a ride as Detroit had ever let loose in a polite society. But drivers who liked to compete on the street in more civilized fashion were more than thrilled by the 1970½ rendition's more cooperative, better-balanced brand of performance.

The new Camaro's improved chassis and better-insulated body meant that, in most cases, that trip was smoother and quieter. And just as thrilling. As *Car Life*'s staff concluded, "Despite the added weight and tougher emissions controls, [the '70½ Z28 is] faster than ever, and in a way that makes the car driveable by anybody."

Inspiration for that claim came beneath the latest Z28's even longer hood. Behind that pointed prow was a new power source, a truly muscular mill with a sports car pedigree. A new option for 1970's Corvette, the 350-cubic-inch LT-1 V-8 replaced the Z28's 302 that year. Beneath fiberglass hoods, the LT-1 was rated at 370 horsepower. As the new heart of the Z28, it advertised at 360 horses. Either way, most bystanders then agreed that the LT-1 was probably the greatest small-block V-8 to yet scream down the pike. With a much wider, more usable powerband than its 302 predecessor, the 360-horsepower 350 was even more responsive—to both full-throttle bursts and slow-speed operation.

1970½ CAMARO Z28

Model availability	2-door sport coupe
Wheelbase	108 inches
Length	188 inches
Width	74.4 inches
Height	50.5 inches
Curb weight	3,580 pounds
Base price	$3,794
Track	61.3/60 (front/rear, in inches)
Wheels	15 × 7
Tires	F60 Goodyear Polyglas
Suspension	independent A-arms, coil springs & stabilizer bar in front; solid axle w/multi-leaf springs & stabilizer bar in back
Steering	recirculating ball
Brakes	power-assisted front discs, rear drums
Engine	360-horsepower 350-cubic-inch V-8
Bore & stroke	4.00 × 3.48 inches
Compression	11:1
Fuel delivery	780-cfm Holley 4-barrel carburetor
Transmission	4-speed manual or Turbo Hydra-Matic automatic
Axle ratio	3.73:1 Positraction

Right: Various glitches helped delay the second-generation Camaro's debut until February 1970, thus the 1970½ reference. Z28 production carried over in grand fashion.

Opposite top: One of the highlights of the new F-body design for 1970 was its lengthened, pointed prow. The Z28's blacked-out grille drew even more attention up front.

Opposite bottom: New 15 × 7 wheels, chrome exhaust tips, and a rear deck spoiler all came standard on the Z28 in 1970.

Above: Chevrolet's LT-1 350 produced 370 horsepower under fiberglass hoods in 1970. It was down-rated to 360 horses for the 1970½ Z28.

Left: Z28 buyers in 1970 could choose between a Muncie four-speed or Turbo Hydra-Matic automatic transmission. The Hurst stick seen here controls the M21 close-ratio four-speed. Additional options included power steering, a tilt wheel, and an AM push-button radio.

Opposite: A compression cut dropped Z28 output down to 330 horsepower for 1971. Front and rear spoilers were standard that year.

Such relatively civilized compatibility allowed engineers to offer the Turbo Hydra-Matic automatic (albeit a beefed-up version with a high-stall torque converter) as a Z28 option for the first time.

Previous models had all been Muncie four-speeds. The M40 Hydra-Matic option cost $290.40 when paired with RPO Z28. The Muncie four-speed, in either M20 wide-ratio or M21 close-ratio form, cost $205.95.

The LT-1's extra 48 cubes were allowed entry into the Z28's engine bay thanks to an SCCA rules change. Previously, destroking a production engine to meet the 305-cubic-inch Trans-Am limit was not allowed. But this left Dodge and Plymouth out of the picture, because no mixing and matching of

Chrysler hardware could bridge the gap between the 273- and 318-cubic-inch Mopar small-blocks. SCCA officials then changed their minds about destroking in 1970, a move that allowed the 340-equipped T/A Challenger and AAR 'Cuda to qualify for Trans-Am competition. With that done, it became only logical at Chevrolet to leave the 302 hybrid behind in favor of the larger 350 small-block.

Like the '69 302, the LT-1 featured big-port heads, solid lifters, rugged four-bolt main bearing caps, a tough forged-steel crank, a high-volume oil pump, and a baffled oil pan with windage tray. TRW impact-extruded pistons again squeezed the air/fuel mixture at an 11:1 ratio. On top, a 780-cfm Holley four-barrel found a home on a revised

aluminum intake that allowed more clearance for lower hood lines. A heavy-duty radiator was included, and a beefier 11-inch clutch replaced the 10.34-inch unit previously used for four-speed models.

Brakes were 11-inch front discs, 9.5-inch rear drums, with power-assist made mandatory. Heavier F41 springs and staggered shocks again appeared and now were joined by a new rear sway bar.

Priced at $572.95 in 1970, RPO Z28 included a rear spoiler, chrome exhaust tips, and new 15 × 7 sport wheels wearing F60 Wide Oval rubber. Special stripes, Z28 identification, a blacked-out grille, and various deluxe trim pieces completed the deal.

1971 CAMARO Z28

Model availability	2-door sport coupe
Wheelbase	108 inches
Length	188 inches
Width	74.4 inches
Height	50.5 inches
Curb weight	3,560 pounds
Base price	$4,005
Track	61.3/60 (front/rear, in inches)
Wheels	15 × 7
Tires	F60 × 15
Suspension	independent A-arms, coil springs & stabilizer bar in front; solid axle w/multi-leaf springs & stabilizer bar in back
Steering	recirculating ball
Brakes	power-assisted front discs, rear drums
Engine	330-horsepower 350-cubic-inch V-8
Bore & stroke	4.00 × 3.48 inches
Compression	9:1
Fuel delivery	Holley 4-barrel carburetor
Transmission	4-speed manual or Turbo Hydra-Matic automatic
Axle ratio	3.73:1 Positraction

1972 CAMARO Z28

Model availability	2-door sport coupe
Wheelbase	108 inches
Length	188 inches
Width	74.4 inches
Height	50.5 inches
Curb weight	3,495 pounds (w/4-speed manual trans)
Price	Z28 Special Performance Package cost $796.15
Track	61.3/60 (front/rear, in inches)
Wheels	15 × 7
Tires	F60 × 15
Suspension	independent A-arms, coil springs & stabilizer bar in front; solid axle w/multi-leaf springs & stabilizer bar in back
Steering	recirculating ball
Brakes	power-assisted front discs, rear drums
Engine	255-horsepower 350-cubic-inch V-8
Bore & stroke	4.00 × 3.48 inches
Compression	9:1
Fuel delivery	Rochester 4-barrel carburetor
Transmission	4-speed manual or Turbo Hydra-Matic automatic
Axle ratio	3.73:1 Positraction

As in 1970 and '71, combining the Rally Sport (RPO Z22) and Z28 packages in 1972 traded the one-piece Camaro front bumper for two small units that did nothing to keep that blacked-out grille out of harm's way. *Courtesy Mecum Auctions*

1971

A compression cut from 11:1 to 9:1 dropped the Z28's output down to 330 horsepower in 1971. Impressions remained exciting as all-important RPO Z28 components again rolled over, but the 350 Turbo Fire's lost horses, working in concert with changing attitudes concerning high performance, meant a dimming future for Chevrolet's Trans-Am pony car. All 1971 Z28s featured front and rear spoilers. RPO Z28 cost $786.75.

Above and right: New net ratings translated into yet another advertised output downturn for 1972's Z28, this time to 255 horsepower. *courtesy Mecum Auctions*

1973 CAMARO Z28

Model availability	2-door sport coupe
Wheelbase	108 inches
Length	188 inches
Width	74.4 inches
Height	50.5 inches
Curb weight	3,689 pounds
Price	Z28 Special Performance Package cost $502.05 w/Type LT coupe
Track	61.3/60 (front/rear, in inches)
Wheels	15 × 7
Tires	F60 × 15
Suspension	independent A-arms, coil springs & stabilizer bar in front; solid axle w/multi-leaf springs & stabilizer bar in back
Steering	recirculating ball
Brakes	power-assisted front discs, rear drums
Engine	245-horsepower 350-cubic-inch V-8
Bore & stroke	4.00 × 3.48 inches
Compression	9:1
Fuel delivery	Holley 4-barrel carburetor on cast-iron intake manifold
Transmission	4-speed manual or Turbo Hydra-Matic automatic
Axle ratio	3.73:1 Positraction

1972

Inhibiting emissions controls limited the Z28's 350 V-8 further. Advertised output dropped to 255 horsepower. Spoilers were dropped from the Z28 package, priced at $769.15.

1973

Civilized hydraulic lifters replaced the solid units used by all previous Z28s in 1973, meaning optional air conditioning could finally enter into the equation. Output for the quieter 350 Turbo Fire was 245 horsepower. Priced at $598.05, RPO Z28 was available that year for the base V-8 Camaro coupe and new Type LT, which replaced the Super Sport. When combined with the Type LT, the Z28 package's price dropped to $502.05 due to various shared features.

1974 CAMARO Z28

Model availability	2-door sport coupe
Wheelbase	108 inches
Length	188 inches
Width	74.4 inches
Height	50.5 inches
Curb weight	3,644 pounds
Price	Z28 Special Performance Package cost $796.15
Track	61.3/60 (front/rear, in inches)
Wheels	15 × 7
Tires	F60 × 15
Suspension	independent A-arms, coil springs & stabilizer bar in front; solid axle w/multi-leaf springs & stabilizer bar in back
Steering	recirculating ball
Brakes	power-assisted front discs, rear drums
Engine	245-horsepower 350-cubic-inch V-8
Bore & stroke	4.00 × 3.48 inches
Compression	9:1
Fuel delivery	4-barrel carburetor
Transmission	4-speed manual or Turbo Hydra-Matic automatic
Axle ratio	3.73:1 Positraction

1974

A mild Camaro makeover and new, prominent graphics made news in 1974, the last year for the original Z. RPO Z28 components carried over unchanged from 1973 to 1974, as did the 350 Turbo Fire's advertised output, thanks to the addition of the more-efficient high energy ignition (HEI).

What killed the original Z-car? "Recent noise level tests conducted by Chevrolet engineers indicate that extensive development and engineering work required to meet the more stringent 1975 sound level standards would not be feasible from a cost/benefit standpoint," said Chevy general manager Robert Lund early that year. Initial plans had the next Z28 on hold until January 1975 with hopes of meeting said standards, but it was not to be. "Although we realize a large segment of owners will be disappointed with our decision, the demise of the Z28 resulted from a legislative trend in [certain] areas, which began in 1972,"

1967–1975 Z28 Production Figures

1967	602
1968	7,199
1969	20,302
1970	8,733
1971	4,862
1972	2,575
1973	11,574
1974	13,802
1975	1

Above: While one mysterious 1975 Z28 was built, the last of the original legacy was sold to the public the previous year. *courtesy Mecum Auctions*

Opposite: Prominent graphics were new in 1974, the final year (save for one mysterious model built in 1975) for Chevy's original Z. *GM*

Lund continued. "By 1978, these codes will require automobile manufacturers to add sound level equipment to all car lines which could result in a cumulative increase in cost to the U.S. consumer of an estimated $100 per car."

That said, a single 1975 Z28 did manage to roll off the Norwood line. How and/or why remains a mystery still.

1967–1974 Z28 V-8s

Year	CID	Bore & Stroke	Horsepower	Torque	CR
1967–1969[1]	302	4.00 × 3.00	290 at 5,800	290 at 4,200	11:1
1970	350	4.00 × 3.48	360 at 6,000	380 at 4,000	11:1
1971	350	4.00 × 3.48	330 at 5,600[2]	360 at 4,000[2]	9:1
1972	350[3]	4.00 × 3.48	255 at 5,600	280 at 4,000	9:1
1973–1974	350[3]	4.00 × 3.48	245 at 5,200	280 at 4,000	9:1

NOTE: CID is cubic inch displacement; CR is compression ratio; bore & stroke in inches
[1]1969 302 V-8 was fitted with 4-bolt main bearing caps; previous blocks featured 2-bolt mains.
[2]Net-ratings were 275 at 5,600 rpm (horsepower) and 300 at 4,000 rpm (torque).
[3]Net-rated

Index

Wide, thin taillamps separated by sheet metal emphasized the first-gen Camaro's width, enhancing its muscular, planted stance.

5

6

Rear fenders were pulled out, giving the car a wider, more muscular flair.

1

Iconic Chevrolet "cowl induction" power bulge hood signified high performance during the muscle car era.

2

Wide grille opening with dual-plane elements (the grille insert is on a different